MW00993552

GACE 177 Paraprofessional Assessment

Teacher Certification Exam

By Sharon Wynne, M.S.
Southern Connecticut State University

"And, while there's no reason yet to panic, I think it's only prudent that we make preparations to panic."

XAMonline, Inc.
Boston

Copyright © 2008 XAMonline, Inc.
All rights reserved. No part of the material protected by this copyright notice may be reproduced or utilized in any form or by any means, electronic or mechanical, including photocopying, recording or by any information storage and retrievable system, without written permission from the copyright holder.

To obtain permission(s) to use the material from this work for any purpose including workshops or seminars, please submit a written request to:

XAMonline, Inc.
21 Orient Ave.
Melrose, MA 02176
Toll Free 1-800-509-4128
Email: info@xamonline.com
Web www.xamonline.com
Fax: 1-781-662-9268

Library of Congress Cataloging-in-Publication Data

Wynne, Sharon A.
GACE Paraprofessional Assessment 177: Teacher Certification / Sharon A. Wynne. 2nd ed.
ISBN 978-1-58197-588-8
1.Paraprofessional 2. Study Guides. 3. GACE
4. Teachers' Certification & Licensure. 5. Careers

Disclaimer:
The opinions expressed in this publication are the sole works of XAMonline and were created independently from the National Education Association, Educational Testing Service, or any State Department of Education, National Evaluation Systems or other testing affiliates.

Between the time of publication and printing, state specific standards as well as testing formats and website information may change that is not included in part or in whole within this product. Sample test questions are developed by XAMonline and reflect similar content as on real tests; however, they are not former tests. XAMonline assembles content that aligns with state standards but makes no claims nor guarantees teacher candidates a passing score. Numerical scores are determined by testing companies such as NES or ETS and then are compared with individual state standards. A passing score varies from state to state.

Printed in the United States of America **œ-1**

GACE: Paraprofessional Assessment 177
ISBN: 978-1-58197-588-8

Table of Contents

SUBAREA II. WRITING

Great Study and Testing Tips!

What to study in order to prepare for the subject assessments is the focus of this study guide but equally important is *how* you study.

You can increase your chances of truly mastering the information by taking some simple but effective steps.

Study Tips:

1. Some foods aid the learning process. Foods such as milk, nuts, seeds, rice, and oats help your study efforts by releasing natural memory enhancers called CCKs (cholecystokinin) composed of tryptophan, choline, and phenylalanine. All of these chemicals enhance the neurotransmitters associated with memory. Before studying, try a light, protein-rich meal of eggs, turkey, and fish. All of these foods release the memory-enhancing chemicals. The better the connections, the more you comprehend.

Likewise, before you take a test, stick to a light snack of energy boosting and relaxing foods. A glass of milk, a piece of fruit, or some peanuts all release various memory-boosting chemicals and help you to relax and focus on the subject at hand.

2. Learn to take great notes. A by-product of our modern culture is that we have grown accustomed to getting our information in short doses (i.e. TV news sound bites or *USA Today*-style newspaper articles.)

Consequently, we've subconsciously trained ourselves to assimilate information better in neat little packages. If you scrawl notes all over the paper, you fragment the flow of the information. Strive for clarity. Newspapers use a standard format to achieve clarity. Your notes can be much clearer through use of proper formatting. A very effective format is called the Cornell Method.

- Take a sheet of loose-leaf lined notebook paper and draw a line all the way down the paper about 1-2" from the left-hand edge.

- Draw another line across the width of the paper about 1-2" up from the bottom. Repeat this process on the reverse side of the page.

Look at the highly effective result. You have ample room for notes, a left-hand margin for special emphasis items or inserting supplementary data from the textbook, a large area at the bottom for a brief summary, and a little rectangular space for just about anything you want.

3. Get the concept, and then the details. Too often we focus on the details and don't gather an understanding of the concept. However, if you simply memorize only dates, places, or names, you may well miss the whole point of the subject.

A key way to understand things is to put them in your own words. If you are working from a textbook, automatically summarize each paragraph in your mind. If you are outlining text, don't simply copy the author's words.

Rephrase them in your own words. You remember your own thoughts and words much better than someone else's, and you subconsciously tend to associate the important details to the core concepts.

4. Ask Why. Pull apart written material paragraph by paragraph and don't forget the captions under the illustrations.

Example: If the heading is "Stream Erosion," flip it around to read "Why do streams erode?" Then answer the questions.

If you train your mind to think in a series of questions and answers, not only will you learn more but you will also lessen the test anxiety because you are used to answering questions.

5. Read for reinforcement and future needs. Even if you only have 10 minutes, put your notes or a book in your hand. Your mind is similar to a computer; you have to input data in order to have it processed. *By reading, you are creating the neural connections for future retrieval.* The more times you read something, the more you reinforce the learning of ideas.

Even if you don't fully understand something on the first pass, *your mind stores much of the material for later recall.*

6. Relax to learn so go into exile. Our bodies respond to an inner clock called biorhythms. Burning the midnight oil works well for some people, but not everyone.

If possible, set aside a particular place to study that is free of distractions. Shut off the television, cell phone, and pager and exile your friends and family during your study period.

If you really are bothered by silence, try background music. Light classical music at a low volume has been shown to aid in concentration.

Music that evokes pleasant emotions without lyrics are highly suggested. Try just about anything by Mozart. It relaxes you.

7. Use arrows, not highlighters. At best, it's difficult to read a page full of yellow, pink, blue, and green streaks.

Try staring at a neon sign for a while and you'll soon see my point; the horde of colors obscures the message.

A quick note: a brief dash of color, an underline, and an arrow pointing to a particular passage are much clearer than a horde of highlighted words.

8. Budget your study time. Although you shouldn't ignore any of the material, ***allocate your available study time in the same ratio that topics may appear on the test.***

Testing Tips:

1. Get smart, play dumb. Don't read anything into the question. Don't assume that the test writer is looking for something other than what is asked. Stick to the question as written and don't read extra things into it.

2. Read the question and all the choices *twice* before answering the question. You may miss something by not carefully reading and then rereading both the question and the answers.

If you really don't have a clue as to the right answer, leave it blank on the first time through. Go on to the other questions as they may provide a clue on how to answer the skipped questions.

If later on, you still can't answer the skipped ones . . . ***Guess.*** The only penalty for guessing is that you *might* get it wrong. Only one thing is certain; if you don't put anything down, you will get it wrong!

3. Turn the question into a statement. Look at the way the questions are worded. The syntax of the question usually provides a clue. Does it seem more familiar as a statement rather than as a question? Does it sound strange?

By turning a question into a statement, you may be able to spot if an answer sounds right, and it may also trigger memories of material you have read.

4. Look for hidden clues. It's actually very difficult to compose multiple-foil (choice) questions without giving away part of the answer in the options presented.

In most multiple-choice questions you can often readily eliminate one or two of the potential answers. This leaves you with only two real possibilities and automatically your odds go to fifty-fifty for very little work.

5. **Trust your instincts.** For every fact that you have read, you subconsciously retain something of that knowledge. On questions that you aren't certain about, go with your basic instincts. **Your first impression on how to answer a question is usually correct.**

6. **Mark your answers directly on the test booklet.** Don't bother trying to fill in the optical scan sheet on the first pass through the test.
Just be very careful not to mismark your answers when you eventually transcribe them to the scan sheet.

7. **Watch the clock!** You have a set amount of time to answer the questions. Don't get bogged down trying to answer a single question at the expense of 10 questions you can more readily answer.

THIS PAGE BLANK

COMPETENCY 1.0 UNDERSTAND THE MEANING OF COMMON VOCABULARY WORDS AND STRATEGIES FOR DERIVING THE MEANING OF UNFAMILIAR WORDS

Skill 1.1 Identify meaning of words or phrases in context

Context clues help readers determine the meaning of words they are not familiar with. The context of a word is the sentence or sentences that surround the word.

Read the following sentences and attempt to determine the meanings of the words in bold print.

> The **luminosity** of the room was so incredible that there was no need for lights.
>
> > If there was no need for lights then one must assume that the word *luminosity* has something to do with giving off light. The definition of *luminosity* is: the emission of light.
>
> Jamie could not understand Joe's feelings. His mood swings made understanding him somewhat of an **enigma.**
>
> > The fact that he could not be understood made him somewhat of a puzzle. The definition of *enigma* is: a mystery or puzzle.

Familiarity with word roots (the basic elements of words) and with prefixes can also help one determine the meanings of unknown words.

Following is a partial list of roots and prefixes. It might be useful to review these.

Root	Meaning	Example
aqua	water	aqualung
astro	stars	astrology
bio	life	biology
carn	meat	carnivorous
circum	around	circumnavigate
geo	earth	geology
herb	plant	herbivorous
mal	bad	malicious
neo	new	neonatal
tele	distant	telescope

Prefix	Meaning	Example
un-	not	unnamed
re-	again	reenter
il-	not	illegible
pre-	before	preset
mis-	incorrectly	misstate
in-	not	informal
anti-	against	antiwar
de-	opposite	derail
post-	after	postwar
ir-	not	irresponsible

Word Forms

Sometimes a very familiar word can appear as a different part of speech. You may have heard that *fraud* involves a criminal misrepresentation, so when it appears as the adjective form *fraudulent* ("He was suspected of fraudulent activities") you can make an educated guess.

You probably know that something out of date is *obsolete;* therefore, when you read about "built-in *obsolescence,*" you can detect the meaning of the unfamiliar word.

Practice Questions: Read the following sentences and determine the meanings of the underlined words.

1. Farmer John got a two-horse plow and went to work. Straight furrows stretched out behind him.

   The word furrows means

   A. long cuts made by plow
   B. vast, open fields
   C. rows of corn
   D. pairs of hitched horses

2. The survivors struggled ahead, shambling through the terrible cold, doing their best not to fall.

   The word shambling means

   A. frozen in place
   B. running
   C. shivering uncontrollably
   D. walking awkwardly

Answers:

1. Answer A is correct. The words "straight" and the expression "stretched out behind him" are your clues.

2. Answer D is correct. The words "ahead" and "through" are your clues.

Sentence Clues

Context clues can appear within the sentence itself, within the preceding and/or following sentence(s), or in the passage as a whole. The context for a word is the written passage that surrounds it. Sometimes the writer offers synonyms—words that have nearly the same meaning.

Often, a writer will actually **define** a difficult or particularly important word for you the first time it appears in a passage. Phrases like *that is, such as, which is,* or *is called* might announce the writer's intention to give just the definition you need. Occasionally, a writer will simply use a synonym (a word that means the same thing) or near-synonym joined by the word *or.* Look at the following examples:

> The *credibility, that is to say the believability,* of the witness was called into question by evidence of previous perjury.

> Nothing would *assuage or lessen* the child's grief.

Punctuation at the sentence level is often a clue to the meaning of a word. Commas, parentheses, quotation marks and dashes tell the reader that a definition is being offered by the writer.

> A tendency toward *hyperbole, extravagant exaggeration*, is a common flaw among persuasive writers.

> Political *apathy - lack of interest* - can lead to the death of the state.

A writer might simply give an **explanation** in other words that you can understand, in the same sentence:

> The *xenophobic* townspeople were *suspicious of every foreigner.*

Writers also explain a word in terms of its opposite at the sentence level:

> His *incarceration* was ended, and he was elated to be *out of jail.*

Adjacent Sentence Clues

The context for a word goes beyond the sentence in which it appears. At times, the writer uses adjacent (adjoining) sentences to present an explanation or definition:

> The 200 dollars for the car repair would have to come out of the *contingency* fund. Fortunately, Angela's father had taught her to keep some *money set aside for just such emergencies.*

Analysis: The second sentence offers a clue to the definition of *contingency* as used in this sentence: "emergencies." Therefore, a fund for contingencies would be money tucked away for unforeseen and/or urgent events.

Entire Passage Clues

On occasion, you must look at an entire paragraph or passage to figure out the definition of a word or term. In the following paragraph, notice how the word *nostalgia* undergoes a form of extended definition throughout the selection rather than in just one sentence.

> The word *nostalgia* links Greek words for "away from home" and "pain." If you're feeling *nostalgic*, then, you are probably in some physical distress or discomfort, suffering from a feeling of alienation and separation from love ones or loved places. *Nostalgia* is that awful feeling you remember the first time you went away to camp or spent the weekend with a friend's family—homesickness, or some condition even more painful than that. But in common use, *nostalgia* has come to have more sentimental associations. A few years back, for example, a *nostalgia* craze had to do with the 1950s. We resurrected poodle skirts and saddle shoes, built new restaurants to look like old ones, and tried to make chicken a la king just as mother probably never made it. In TV situation comedies, we recreated a pleasant world that probably never existed and relished our *nostalgia*, longing for a homey, comfortable lost time.

Skill 1.2 Recognize synonyms and antonyms for words

Synonyms are words that have similar meanings. Sometimes, synonyms can be used to in place of another word to make a draft more appealing or descriptive. As teachers, you should encourage your students to use appropriate synonyms when drafting or revising their work to expand a written work's interest and imagery. Paper or computer thesauruses are helpful in incorporating synonyms into one's writing.

Examples of synonyms:
Happy – gay, joyful, ecstatic, content, cheerful
Angry – irritated, fuming, livid, irate, annoyed
Beautiful - gorgeous, attractive, striking

However, you will want to alert students that sometimes one word cannot be simply replaced by another just because it was listed as a synonym. Sometimes the meaning or the connotation will vary somewhat. For example, in the sentence, "Harold was *angry* when his brother spilled finger paint on his book report," replacing *angry* with *fuming* would be a better choice than *annoyed* as the words describe the situation a little differently. As you work with students, help students expand their vocabularies so they know which synonyms to use.

Antonyms are words that have opposite meanings. Like synonyms, thesauruses will help students identify words that are antonyms.

Examples of antonyms:
Sad – cheerful, delighted
Angry - calm, content
Beautiful – ugly, repulsive, hideous

Skill 1.3 Recognize correct use of commonly misused words (e.g., their/they're, to/too)

Students frequently encounter problems with homonyms—words that are spelled and pronounced the same as another but that have different meanings such as *mean*, a verb, "to intend"; *mean* an adjective, "unkind"; and *mean* a noun or adjective, "average." These words are actually both homonyms and homographs (written the same way).

A similar phenomenon that causes trouble is heteronyms (also sometimes called heterophones), words that are spelled the same but have different pronunciations and meanings (in other words, they are homographs that differ in pronunciation or, technically, homographs that are not homophones).

For example, the homographs *desert* (abandon) and *desert* (arid region) are heteronyms (pronounced differently); but *mean* (intend) and *mean* (average) are not. They are pronounced the same, or are homonyms.

Another similar occurrence in English is the capitonym, a word that is spelled the same but has different meanings when it is capitalized and may or may not have different pronunciations. Example: *polish* (to make shiny) and *Polish* (from Poland).

Find more troublesome words at
An English Homophone Dictionary
http://www.earlham.edu/~peters/writing/homofone.htm

Some of the most troubling homonyms are those that are spelled differently but sound the same. Examples: *its* (3d person singular neuter pronoun) and *it's* ("it is"); *there, their* (3d person plural pronoun) and *they're* ("they are"). Others: *to, too, two.*

Some homonyms/homographs are particularly complicated and troubling. Fluke, for instance is a fish, a flatworm, the end parts of an anchor, the fins on a whale's tail, and a stroke of luck.

Commonly Misused Words

Accept is a verb meaning to receive or to tolerate. **Except** is usually a preposition meaning excluding. Except is also a verb meaning to exclude.

Advice is a noun meaning recommendation. **Advise** is a verb meaning to recommend.

Affect is usually a verb meaning to influence. **Effect** is usually a noun meaning result. Effect can also be a verb meaning to bring about.

An **allusion** is an indirect reference. An **illusion** is a misconception or false impression.

Add is a verb to mean to put together. **Ad** is a noun that is the abbreviation for the word advertisement.

Ain't is a common nonstandard contraction for the contraction aren't.

Allot is a verb meaning to distribute. **A lot** can be an adverb that means often, or to a great degree. It can also mean a large quantity.

Allowed is an adjective that means permitted. **Aloud** is an adverb that means audibly.

Bare is an adjective that means naked or exposed. It can also indicate a minimum. As a noun, **bear** is a large mammal. As a verb, bear means to carry a heavy burden.

Capitol refers to a city, capitol to a building where lawmakers meet. **Capital** also refers to wealth or resources.

A **chord** is a noun that refers to a group of musical notes. **Cord** is a noun meaning rope or a long electrical line.

Compliment is a noun meaning a praising or flattering remark. **Complement** is a noun that means something that completes or makes perfect.

Climactic is derived from climax, the point of greatest intensity in a series or progression of events. **Climatic** is derived from climate; it refers to meteorological conditions.

Discreet is an adjective that means tactful or diplomatic; **discrete** is an adjective that means separate or distinct.

Dye is a noun or verb used to indicate artificially coloring something. **Die** is a verb that means to pass away. Die is also a noun that means a cube-shaped game piece.

Elicit is a verb meaning to bring out or to evoke. **Illicit** is an adjective meaning unlawful

Emigrate means to leave one country or region to settle in another. **Immigrate** means to enter another country and reside there.

Hoard is a verb that means to accumulate or store up. **Horde** is a large group.

Lead /lēd/ is a verb that means to guide or serve as the head of. It is also a noun /lĕd/ that is a type of metal.

Medal is a noun that means an award that is strung round the neck. **Meddle** is a verb that means to involve oneself in a matter without right or invitation. **Metal** is an element such as silver or gold. **Mettle** is a noun meaning toughness or guts.

Morning is a noun indicating the time between midnight and midday. **Mourning** is a verb or noun pertaining to the period of grieving after a death.

Past is a noun meaning a time before now (past, present and future). **Passed** is past tense of the verb "to pass."

Piece is a noun meaning a portion. **Peace** is a noun meaning the opposite of war.

Peak is a noun meaning the tip or height to reach the highest point. **Peek** is a verb that means to take a brief look. **Pique** is a verb meaning to incite or raise interest.

Principal is a noun meaning the head of a school or an organization or a sum of money. **Principle** is a noun meaning a basic truth or law.

Rite is a noun meaning a special ceremony. **Right** is an adjective meaning correct or direction. **Write** is a verb meaning to compose in writing.

Than is a conjunction used in comparisons; **then** is an adverb denoting time. That pizza is more than I can eat. Tom laughed, and then we recognized him.

Here's a mnemonic device to remember the difference. *Than* is used to *compare*; both words have the letter *a* in them. *Then* tells *when*; both are spelled the same, except for the first letter.

There is an adverb specifying place; it is also an expletive. Adverb: Sylvia is lying there unconscious. Expletive: *There* are two plums left. **Their** is a possessive pronoun. **They're** is a contraction of they are. Fred and Jane finally washed *their* car. *They're* later than usual today.

To is a preposition; **too** is an adverb; **two** is a number.

Your is a possessive pronoun; **you're** is a contraction of you are.

Other Confusing Words

Among is a preposition to be used with three or more items. **Between** is to be used with two items.

> Between you and me, I cannot tell the difference among those three Johnson sisters.

As is a subordinating conjunction used to introduce a subordinating clause; **like** is a preposition and is followed by a noun or a noun phrase.

> As I walked to the lab, I realized that the recent experiment findings were much like those we found last year.

Can is a verb that means to be able. **May** is a verb that means to have permission. They are only interchangeable in cases of possibility.

> I can lift 250 pounds.
> May I go to Alex's house?

Lie is an intransitive verb meaning to recline or rest on a surface. Its principal parts are lie, lay, lain. **Lay** is a transitive verb meaning to put or place. Its principal parts are lay, laid.

> Birds lay eggs.
> I lie down for bed around 10 p.m.

Set is a transitive verb meaning to put or to place. Its principal parts are set, set, set. **Sit** is an intransitive verb meaning to be seated. Its principal parts are sit, sat, sat.

I set my backpack down near the front door.
They sat in the park until the sun went down.

Problem Phrases

Correct	**Incorrect**
Anyway	Anyways
Come to see me	Come and see me
Could have, would have, should have	Could of, would of, should of
Couldn't care less	Could care less
En route	In route
For all intents and purposes	For all intensive purposes
Regardless	Irregardless
Second, Third	Secondly, Thirdly
Supposed to	Suppose to
Toward	Towards
Try to	Try and
Used to	Use to

COMPETENCY 2.0 UNDERSTAND HOW TO INTERPRET AND ANALYZE A WIDE RANGE OF TEXTS

Skill 2.1 Identify the main idea of a passage

The main idea of a passage or paragraph is the basic message, idea, point concept, or meaning that the author wants to convey to you, the reader. Understanding the main idea of a passage or paragraph is the key to understanding the more subtle components of the author's message. The main idea is what is being said about a topic or subject. Once you have identified the basic message, you will have an easier time answering other questions that test critical skills.

Main ideas are either *stated* or *implied.* A *stated main idea* is explicit: it is directly expressed in a sentence or two in the paragraph or passage. An *implied main idea* is suggested by the overall reading selection. In the first case, you need not pull information from various points in the paragraph or passage in order to form the main idea because it is already stated by the author. If a main idea is implied, however, you must formulate, in your own words, a main idea statement by condensing the overall message contained in the material itself.

Practice Question: Read the following passage and select an answer

> Sometimes too much of a good thing can become a very bad thing indeed. In an earnest attempt to consume a healthy diet, dietary supplement enthusiasts have been known to overdose. Vitamin C, for example, long thought to help people ward off cold viruses, is currently being studied for its possible role in warding off cancer and other disease that cases tissue degeneration. Unfortunately, an overdose of vitamin C—more than 10,000 mg—on a daily basis can cause nausea and diarrhea. Calcium supplements, commonly taken by women, are helpful in warding off osteoporosis. More than just a few grams a day, however, can lead to stomach upset and even kidney and bladder stones. Niacin, proven useful in reducing cholesterol levels, can be dangerous in large doses to those who suffer from heart problems, asthma or ulcers.

The main idea expressed in this paragraph is:

A. supplements taken in excess can be a bad thing indeed
B. dietary supplement enthusiasts have been known to overdose
C. vitamins can cause nausea, diarrhea, and kidney or bladder stones
D. people who take supplements are preoccupied with their health

Answer: Answer A is a paraphrase of the first sentence and provides a general framework for the rest of the paragraph: Excess supplement intake is bad. The rest of the paragraph discusses the consequences of taking too many vitamins. Options B and C refer to major details, and Option D introduces the idea of preoccupation, which is not included in this paragraph.

Skill 2.2 Recognize supporting ideas in a passage

Supporting details are examples, facts, ideas, illustrations, cases and anecdotes used by a writer to explain, expand on, and develop the more general main idea. A writer's choice of supporting materials is determined by the nature of the topic being covered. Supporting details are specifics that relate directly to the main idea. Writers select and shape material according to their purposes.

An advertisement writer seeking to persuade the reader to buy a particular running shoe, for instance, will emphasize only the positive characteristics of the shoe for advertisement copy. A columnist for a running magazine, on the other hand, might list the good and bad points about the same shoe in an article recommending appropriate shoes for different kind of runners. Both major details (those that directly support the main idea), and minor details (those that provide interesting, but not always essential, information) help create a well-written and fluid passage.

In the following paragraph, the sentences in **bold print** provide a skeleton of a paragraph on the benefits of recycling. The sentences in bold are generalizations that by themselves do not explain the need to recycle. The sentences in *italics* add details to SHOW the general points in bold. Notice how the supporting details help you understand the necessity for recycling.

> **While one day recycling may become mandatory in all states, right now it is voluntary in many communities.** *Those of us who participate in recycling are amazed by how much material is recycled.* **For many communities, the blue-box recycling program has had an immediate effect.** *By just recycling glass, aluminum cans, and plastic bottles, we have reduced the volume of disposable trash by one third, thus extending the useful life of local landfills by over a decade. Imagine the difference if those dramatic results were achieved nationwide.* **The amount of reusable items we thoughtlessly dispose of is staggering.** *For example, Americans dispose of enough steel everyday to supply Detroit car manufacturers for three months. Additionally, we dispose of enough aluminum annually to rebuild the nation's air fleet. These statistics, available from the Environmental Protection Agency (EPA), should encourage all of us to watch what we throw away.* **Clearly, recycling in our homes and in our communities directly improves the environment.**

Notice how the author's supporting examples enhance the message of the paragraph and relate to the author's thesis noted above. If you only read the bold-faced sentences, you have a glimpse at the topic. This paragraph, however, is developed through numerous details creating specific images: *reduced the volume of disposable trash by one-third; extended the useful life of local landfills by over a decade; enough steel everyday to supply Detroit car manufacturers for three months; enough aluminum to rebuild the nation's air fleet.* If the writer had merely written a few general sentences, as those shown in bold face, you would not fully understand the vast amount of trash involved in recycling or the positive results of current recycling efforts.

Skill 2.3 Draw inferences and conclusions from directly stated content

An **inference** is sometimes called an "educated guess" because it requires that you go beyond the strictly obvious to create additional meaning by taking the text one logical step further. Inferences and conclusions are based on the content of the passage—that is, on what the passage says or how the writer says it—and are derived by reasoning.

Inference is an essential and automatic component of most reading. For example, in making educated guesses about the meaning of unknown words, the author's main idea or whether with the author is writing with a bias. Such is the essence of inference: you use your own ability to reason in order to figure out what the writer implies. As a reader, then, you must often logically extend meaning that is only implied.

Consider the following example. Assume you are an employer, and you are reading over the letters of reference submitted by a prospective employee for the position of clerk/typist in your real estate office. The position requires the applicant to be neat, careful, trustworthy, and punctual. You come across this letter of reference submitted by an applicant:

> To whom it may concern,
>
> Todd Finley has asked me to write a letter of reference for him. I am well qualified to do so because he worked for me for three months last year. His duties included answering the phone, greeting the public, and producing some simple memos and notices on the computer. Although Todd initially had few computer skills and little knowledge of telephone etiquette, he did acquire some during his stay with us. Todd's manner of speaking, both on the telephone and with the clients who came to my establishment, could be described as casual. He was particularly effective when communicating with peers. Please contact me by telephone if you wish to have further information about my experience.

Here the writer implies, rather than openly states, the main idea. This letter calls attention to itself because there's a problem with its tone. A truly positive letter would say something like "I have distinct honor to recommend Todd Finley." Here, however, the letter simply verifies that Todd worked in the office. Second, the praise is obviously lukewarm. For example, the writer says that Todd "was particularly effective when communicating with peers." An educated guess translates that statement into a nice way of saying Todd was not serious about his communication with clients.

In order to draw **inferences** and make **conclusions**, a reader must use prior knowledge and apply it to the current situation. A conclusion or inference is never stated. You must rely on your common sense.

Practice Questions: Read the following passages and select an answer

1. The Smith family waited patiently around carousel number 7 for their luggage to arrive. They were exhausted after their five-hour trip and were anxious to get to their hotel. After about an hour, they realized that they no longer recognized any of the other passengers' faces. Mrs. Smith asked the person who appeared to be in charge if they were at the right carousel. The man replied, "Yes, this is it, but we finished unloading that baggage almost half an hour ago."

   From the man's response we can infer that
   A. The Smiths were ready to go to their hotel.
   B. The Smith's luggage was lost.
   C. The man had their luggage.
   D. They were at the wrong carousel.

2. Tim Sullivan had just turned 15. As a birthday present, his parents had given him a guitar and a certificate for ten guitar lessons. He had always shown a love of music and a desire to learn an instrument. Tim began his lessons and before long he was making up his own songs. At the music studio, Tim met Josh, who played the piano, and Roger, whose instrument was the saxophone. They all shared the same dream, to start a band and each was praised by his teacher as having real talent.

   From this passage one can infer that
   A. Tim, Roger and Josh are going to start their own band.
   B. Tim is going to give up his guitar lessons.
   C. Tim, Josh, and Roger will no longer be friends.
   D. Josh and Roger are going to start their own band.

Answers:

1. Choice B is the correct answer. Since the Smiths were still waiting for their luggage, we know that they were not yet ready to go to their hotel. From the man's response, we know that they were not at the wrong carousel and that he did not have their luggage. Therefore, though not directly stated, it appears that their luggage was lost.

2. Choice C is the correct answer. Given the facts that Tim wanted to be a musician and start his own band, after meeting others who shared the same dreams, we can infer that they joined together in an attempt to make their dreams become a reality.

Skill 2.4 Recognize cause-and-effect relationships in a passage

A cause is the necessary source of a particular outcome. If a writer were addressing the question "How will the new tax laws affect small businesses?" or "Why has there been such political unrest in Somalia?" he or she would use cause and effect as an organizational pattern to structure their response. In the first case, the writer would emphasize effects of the tax legislation as they apply to owners of small businesses. In the second, the writer would focus on causes for the current political situation in Somalia.

Some word clues that identify a cause-effect passage are: *accordingly, as a result, therefore, because, consequently, hence, in short, thus, then, due to* and *so on.*

> Sample passage:
> Simply put, inflation is an increase in price levels. It happens when a government prints more currency than is already in circulation, and there is, consequently, additional money available for the same amount of good or services. There might be multiple reasons for a government to crank up the printing presses. A war, for instance, could cause an immediate need for steel. A national disaster might create a sudden need for social services. To get the money it needs, a government can raise taxes, borrow, or print more currency. However, raising taxes and borrowing are not always plausible options.

Analysis: The paragraph starts with a definition and proceeds to examine a causal chain. The words *consequently*, *reasons* and *cause* provide the clues.

Explicit Cause and Effect

General Hooker failed to anticipate General Lee's bold flanking maneuver. As a result, Hooker's army was nearly routed by a smaller force.

Mindy forgot to bring the lunch her father had packed for her. Consequently, she had to borrow money from her friends at school during lunch period.

Implicit Cause and Effect

The engine in Lisa's airplane began to sputter. She quickly looked below for a field in which to land.

Luther ate the creamed shrimp that had been sitting in the sun for hours. Later that night, he was so sick he had to be rushed to the hospital.

Skill 2.5 Distinguish between fact and opinion in written texts

Facts are statements that are verifiable. Opinions are statements that must be supported in order to be accepted such as beliefs, values, judgments or feelings. Facts are objective statements used to support subjective opinions.

For example, "Jane is a bad girl" is an opinion. However, "Jane hit her sister with a baseball bat" is a *fact* upon which the opinion is based. Judgments are opinions—decisions or declarations based on observation or reasoning that express approval or disapproval. Facts report what has happened or exists and come from observation, measurement, or calculation. Facts can be tested and verified whereas opinions and judgments cannot. They can only be supported with facts.

Most statements cannot be so clearly distinguished. "I believe that Jane is a bad girl" is a fact. The speaker knows what he/she believes. However, it obviously includes a judgment that could be disputed by another person who might believe otherwise. Judgments are not usually so firm. They are, rather, plausible opinions that provoke thought or lead to factual development.

Joe DiMaggio, a Yankees' center-fielder, was replaced by Mickey Mantle in 1952.

This is a fact. If necessary, evidence can be produced to support this.

First year players are more ambitious than seasoned players.

This is an opinion. There is no proof to support that everyone feels this way.

Practice Questions: Decide if the statement is fact or opinion

1. The Inca were a group of Indians who ruled an empire in South America.

   A. fact
   B. opinion

2. The Inca were clever.

   A. fact
   B. opinion

3. The Inca built very complex systems of bridges.

   A. fact
   B. opinion

Answers:

1. The correct answer is A. Research can prove this to be true.

2. The correct answer is B. It is doubtful that all people who have studied the Inca agree with this statement. Therefore, no proof is available.

3. The correct answer is A. As with question number one, research can prove this to be true.

Skill 2.6 Identify literary elements (e.g., character, setting, plot, climax)

Most works of fiction contain a common set of elements that make them come alive to readers. In a way, even though writers do not consciously think about each of these elements as story elements when they sit down to write, all stories essentially contain these "markers" that make them the stories that they are. But, even though all stories have these elements, they are a lot like fingerprints: Each story's elements are just a bit different.

Story Elements

Let's look at a few of the most commonly discussed elements. The most commonly discussed story element in fiction is **plot**. Plot is the series of events in a story. Typically, but not always, plot moves in a predictable fashion:

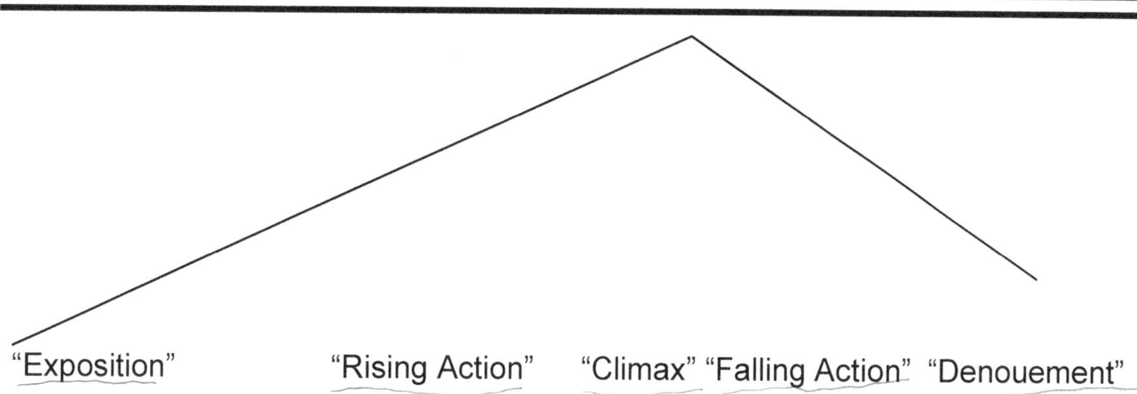

"Exposition" "Rising Action" "Climax" "Falling Action" "Denouement"

Exposition is where characters and their situations are introduced. *Rising action* is the point at which conflict starts to occur. *Climax* is the highest point of conflict, often a turning point. *Falling action* is the result of the climax. *Denouement* is the final resolution of the plot.

Character is another commonly studied story element. We will often find in stories heroes, villains, comedic characters, dark characters, and more. When we examine the characters of a story, we look to see who they are and how their traits contribute to the story. Often, because of their characteristics, plot elements become more interesting. For example, authors will pair unlikely characters together somehow that, in turn, creates specific conflict.

The **setting** of a story is the place or location where it occurs. Often, the specific place is not as important as some of the specifics about the setting. For example, the setting of *The Great Gatsby*, New York, is not as significant as the fact that it takes place amid incredible wealth. Conversely, *The Grapes of Wrath*, although taking place in Oklahoma and California, has a more significant setting of poverty. In fact, as the story takes place *around* other migrant workers, the setting is even more significant. In a way, the setting serves as a reason for various conflicts to occur.

Themes of stories are the underlying messages, above and beyond all plot elements, that writers want to convey. Very rarely will one find that good literature is without a theme—or a lesson, message, or ideal. The best writers in the English language all seem to want to convey something about human nature or the world, and they turn to literature in order to do that. Common themes in literature are jealousy, money, love, human against corporation or government These themes are never explicitly stated; rather, they are the result of the portrayal of characters, settings, and plots. Readers get the message even if the theme is not directly mentioned.

Finally, the **mood** of a story is the atmosphere or attitude the writer conveys through descriptive language. Often, mood fits in nicely with theme and setting. For example, in Edgar Allen Poe's stories, we often find a mood of horror and darkness. We get that from the descriptions of characters and the setting, as well as from specific plot elements. Mood simply helps us better understand the writer's theme and intentions through descriptive, stylistic language.

Imagery can be described as a word or sequence of words that refers to any sensory experience—that is, anything that can be seen, tasted, smelled, heard, or felt on the skin or fingers. While writers of prose may also use these devices, it is most distinctive of poetry. The poet intends to make an experience available to the reader. In order to do that, he/she must appeal to one of the senses. The most-often-used one, of course, is the visual sense. The poet will deliberately paint a scene in such a way that the reader can see it. However, the purpose is not simply to stir the visceral feeling but also to stir the emotions.

A good example is *The Piercing Chill* by Taniguchi Buson (1715-1783):

The piercing chill I feel:
My dead wife's comb, in our bedroom,
Under my heel . . .

In only a few short words, the reader can feel many things: the shock that might come from touching the corpse, a literal sense of death, the contrast between her death, and the memories he has of her when she was alive. Imagery might be defined as speaking of the abstract in concrete terms, a powerful device in the hands of a skillful poet.

A **symbol** is an object or action that can be observed with the senses in addition to its suggesting many other things. The lion is a symbol of courage; the cross a symbol of Christianity; the swastika a symbol of Nazi Germany. These can almost be defined as metaphors because society agrees on the one-to-one meaning of them.

Symbols used in literature are usually of a different sort. They tend to be private and personal; their significance is only evident in the context of the work where they are used. A good example is the huge pair of spectacles on a sign board in Fitzgerald's *The Great Gatsby*. They are interesting as a part of the landscape, but they also symbolize divine myopia. A symbol can certainly have more than one meaning, and the meaning may be as personal as the memories and experiences of the particular reader. In analyzing a poem or a story, it's important to identify the symbols and their possible meanings.

Looking for symbols is often challenging, especially for novice poetry readers. However, these suggestions may be useful: First, pick out all the references to concrete objects such as a newspaper, black cats, or the like. Note any that the poet emphasizes by describing in detail, by repeating, or by placing at the very beginning or ending of a poem. Ask: what is the poem about? What does it add up to? Paraphrase the poem and determine whether or not the meaning depends upon certain concrete objects. Then ponder what the concrete object symbolizes in this particular poem. Look for a character with the name of a prophet who does little but utter prophecy or a trio of women who resemble the Three Fates. A symbol may be a part of a person's body such as the eye of the murder victim in Poe's story *The Tell-Tale Heart* or a look, a voice, or a mannerism.

Some things a symbol is not: an abstraction such as truth, death, and love; in narrative, a well-developed character who is not at all mysterious; the second term in a metaphor. In Emily Dickenson's *The Lightning Is a Yellow Fork*, the symbol is the lightning, not the fork.

An **allusion** is like a symbol, and the two sometimes tend to run together. An allusion is defined by Merriam Webster's *Encyclopedia of Literature* as "an implied reference to a person, event, thing, or a part of another text." Allusions are based on the assumption that there is a common body of knowledge shared by poet and reader and that a reference to that body of knowledge will be immediately understood. Allusions to the Bible and classical mythology are common in western literature on the assumption that they will be immediately understood. The use of allusion is a sort of shortcut for poets. They can use an economy of words and count on meaning to come from the reader's own experience.

COMPETENCY 3.0 UNDERSTAND HOW TO INTERPRET GRAPHIC INFORMATION

Skill 3.1 Interpret information from tables, diagrams, charts, and graphs

Complex numerical information or detailed processes are often better expressed in a visual form. Sometimes, graphic information can be presented independently while at other times it supplements text to facilitate comprehension. To determine accurate relationships, students should be able to interpret the data and must first learn how to read the tables, diagrams, charts, and graphs.

Tables

To interpret data in tables, we read across rows and down columns. Each item of interest has different data points listed under different column headings.

Table 1. Sample Purchase Order

Item	Unit	$/Unit	Qty.	Tot. $
Coffee	lb.	2.79	45	125.55
Milk	gal.	1.05	72	75.60
Sugar	lb.	0.23	150	34.50

In Table 1, the first column on the left contains the items in a purchase order. The other columns contain data about each item labeled with column headings. The second column from the left gives the unit of measurement for each item, the third column gives the price per unit, the fourth column gives the quantity of each item ordered, and the fifth column gives the total cost of each item.

Examples: Use Table 1 to answer the following questions.

1. What does the 1.05 value in the table represent?

   Answer: Price in dollars per gallon of milk.

2. What is the total cost of the purchase order?

   Answer: $235.65

3. How many combined pounds of coffee and sugar does this purchase order purchase?

   Answer: 195 lbs.

Quantitative data is often easily presented in graphs and charts in many content areas. However, if students are unable to decipher the graph, their use becomes limited. Since information can clearly be displayed in a graph or chart form, accurate interpretation of the information is an important skill for students.

For graphs, students should be taught to evaluate all the features of the graph, by starting with the main title. Next they should consider what the horizontal axis represents and what the vertical axis represents. Also, students should locate and evaluate the graph's key (if there is one) in case there is more than one variable on the graph. For example, line graphs are often used to plot data from a scientific experiment. If more than one variable was used, a key or legend would indicate what each line on the line graph represented. Then, once students have evaluated the axes and titles, they can begin to assess the results of the experiment.

For charts (such as a pie chart), the process is similar to interpreting bar or line graphs. The key which depicts what each section of the pie chart represents is very important to interpreting the pie chart. Be sure to provide students with lots of assistance and practice with reading and interpreting graphs and charts so their experience with and confidence in reading them develops.

Example: A survey asked five elementary school students to list the number and type of pets they had at home. The first student had three dogs and three fish. The second student had two cats and one dog. The third student had three fish and two dogs. The fourth student had one rabbit, two cats, and one dog. The fifth student had no pets.

Construct a data table and line graph that represents the survey information.

Solution: The following is a table that appropriately represents the data.

Student #	# of Dogs	# of Cats	# of Fish	# of Rabbits	Total # of Pets
1	3	0	3	0	6
2	1	2	0	0	3
3	2	0	3	0	5
4	1	2	0	1	4
5	0	0	0	0	0

The following is a line graph that appropriately represents the total number of pets each student has.

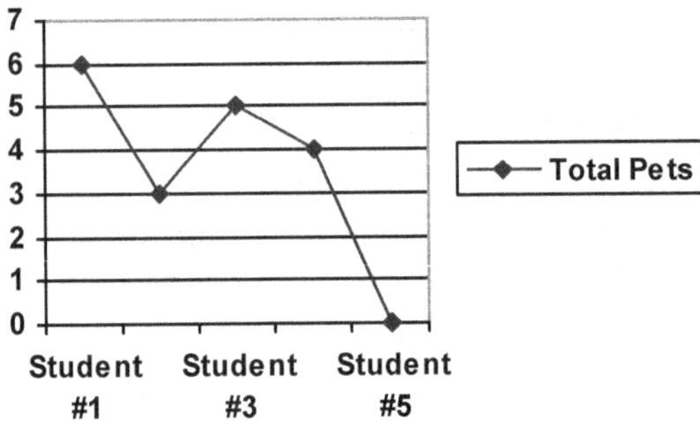

See also Skill 9.1.

Skill 3.2 Recognize appropriate use of graphic formats to represent written information

Writers employ a number of devices, both in text and in pictures, to supplement their informational and technical texts so that readers clearly understand the important ideas.

Tables: Tables depict exact numbers and other data in rows and columns. Those that simply store descriptive information in a form available for general use are called repository tables. They usually contain primary data, which simply summarize raw data. They are not intended to analyze the data, so any analysis is left to the reader or user of the table. A good example of a repository table would be a report of birth statistics by the federal Health and Human Services Department.

An analytical table, on the other hand, is constructed from some sort of analysis of primary or secondary data, possibly from a repository table or from the raw data itself. An example of an analytical table would be one that compares birth statistics in 1980 to birth statistics in 2005 for the country at large. It might also break the data down into comparisons by state.

Graphs: Graphs depict trends, movements, distributions, and cycles more readily than tables. While graphs can present statistics in a more interesting and comprehensible form than tables, they are less accurate. For this reason, the two will often be shown together.

Maps: While the most obvious use for maps is to locate places geographically, they can also show specific geographic features such as roads, mountains, and rivers. They can also show information according to geographic distribution such as population, housing, or manufacturing centers.

Illustrations: A wide range of illustrations, such as pictures, drawings, and diagrams, may be used to illuminate the text in a document. They may also be a part of a graphic layout designed to make the page more attractive.

Some possibilities for the analysis of data whether presented in tables, charts, graphs, maps, or other illustrations are as follow:

- Qualitative descriptions: Would drawing conclusions about the quality of a particular treatment or course of action be revealed by the illustration?
- Quantitative descriptions: How much do the results of one particular treatment or course of action differ from another one, and is that variation significant?
- Classification: Is worthwhile information derived from breaking the information down into classifications?
- Estimations: Is it possible to estimate future performance based on the information in the illustration?
- Comparisons: Is it useful to make comparisons based on the data?
- Relationships. Are relationships between components revealed by the scrutiny of the data?
- Cause-and-effect relationships: Is it suggested by the data that there were cause-and-effect relationships that were not previously apparent?
- Mapping and modeling: If the data were mapped and a model drawn up, would the point of the document be demonstrated or refuted?

Questions to ask regarding an illustration: Why is it in this document? What was the writer's purpose in putting it in the document and why at this particular place? Does it make a point clearer? What implications are inherent in a table that shows birth statistics in all states or even in some selected states? What does that have to do with the point and purpose of this piece of writing? Is there adequate preparation in the text for the inclusion of the illustration? Does the illustration underscore or clarify any of the points made in the text? Is there a clear connection between the illustration and the subject matter of the text?

SAMPLE TEST: READING

Read the passages and answer the questions that follow.

This writer has often been asked to tutor hospitalized children with cystic fibrosis. While undergoing all the precautionary measures to see these children (i.e. scrubbing thoroughly and donning sterilized protective gear- for the child's protection), she has often wondered why their parents subject these children to the pressures of schooling and trying to catch up on what they have missed because of hospitalization, which is a normal part of cystic fibrosis patients' lives. These children undergo so many tortuous treatments a day that it seems cruel to expect them to learn as normal children do, especially with their life expectancies being as short as they are.

1. What is meant by the word "precautionary" in the second sentence? (Skill 1.1, Average Rigor)

A. Careful
B. Protective
C. Medical
D. Sterilizing

2. What is the main idea of this passage? (Skill 2.1, Rigorous)

A. There is a lot of preparation involved in visiting a, patient of cystic fibrosis.
B. Children with cystic fibrosis are incapable of living normal lives.
C. Certain concessions should be made for children with cystic fibrosis.
D. Children with cystic fibrosis die young.

3. What is the author's tone? (Skill 2.3, Rigorous)

A. Sympathetic
B. Cruel
C. Disbelieving
D. Cheerful

4. How is the author so familiar with the procedures used when visiting a child with cystic fibrosis? (Skill 2.3, Average Rigor)

A. She has read about it.
B. She works in a hospital.
C. She is the parent of one.
D. She often tutors them.

5. **What is the author's purpose? (Skill 2.3, Rigorous)**

   A. To inform
   B. To entertain
   C. To describe
   D. To narrate

6. **Is there evidence of bias in this paragraph? (Skill 2.3, Easy)**

   A. Yes
   B. No

7. **Does the author present an argument that is valid or invalid concerning the schooling of children with cystic fibrosis? (Skill 2.4, Rigorous)**

   A. Valid
   B. Invalid

8. **The author states that it is "cruel" to expect children with cystic fibrosis to learn as "normal" children do. Is this a fact or an opinion? (Skill 2.5, Easy)**

   A. Fact
   B. Opinion

9. **What type of organizational pattern is the author using? (Skill 2.6, Easy)**

   A. Classification
   B. Explanation
   C. Comparison and contrast
   D. Cause and effect

10. **What kind of relationship is found within the last sentence which starts with "These children undergo..."and ends with "...as short as they are"? (Skill 2.6, Average Rigor)**

   A. Addition
   B. Explanation
   C. Generalization
   D. Classification

Disciplinary practices have been found to affect diverse areas of child development such as the acquisition of moral values, obedience to authority, and performance at school. Even though the dictionary has a specific definition of the word "discipline," it is still open to interpretation by people of different cultures.

There are four types of disciplinary styles: assertion of power, withdrawal of love, reasoning, and permissiveness. Assertion of power involves the use of force to discourage unwanted behavior. Withdrawal of love involves making the love of a parent conditional on a child's good behavior. Reasoning involves persuading the child to behave one way rather than another. Permissiveness involves allowing the child to do as he or she pleases and face the consequences of his/her actions.

11. What is the meaning of the word "diverse" in the first sentence? (Skill 1.1, Average Rigor)

A. Many
B. Related to children
C. Disciplinary
D. Moral

12. What is the main idea of this passage? (Skill 2.1, Average Rigor)

A. Different people have different ideas of what discipline is.
B. Permissiveness is the most widely used disciplinary style.
C. Most people agree on their definition of discipline.
D. There are four disciplinary styles.

13. Name the four types of disciplinary styles. (Skill 2.2, Easy)

A. Reasoning, power assertion, morality, and permissiveness.
B. Morality, reasoning, permissiveness, and withdrawal of love.
C. Withdrawal of love, permissiveness, assertion of power, and reasoning.
D. Permissiveness, morality, reasoning, and power assertion.

14. What does the technique of reasoning involve? (Skill 2.3, Rigorous)

A. Persuading the child to behave in a certain way.
B. Allowing the child to do as he/she pleases.
C. Using force to discourage unwanted behavior.
D. Making love conditional on good behavior.

15. What is the author's purpose in writing this? (Skill 2.3, Rigorous)

A. To describe
B. To narrate
C. To entertain
D. To inform

16. Is this passage biased? (Skill 2.3, Average Rigor)

A. Yes
B. No

17. What is the author's tone? (Skill 2.3, Rigorous)

A. Disbelieving
B. Angry
C. Informative
D. Optimistic

18. From reading this passage we can conclude that (Skill 2.3, Rigorous)

A. The author is a teacher.
B. The author has many children.
C. The author has written a book about discipline.
D. The author has done a lot of research on discipline.

19. The author states that "assertion of power involves the use of force to discourage unwanted behavior." Is this a fact or an opinion? (Skill 2.5, Average Rigor)

A. Fact
B. Opinion

20. What organizational structure is used in the first sentence of the second paragraph? (Skill 2.6, Easy)

A. Addition
B. Explanation
C. Definition
D. Simple listing

21. What is the overall organizational pattern of this passage? (Skill 2.6, Rigorous)

A. Generalization
B. Cause and effect
C. Addition
D. Summary

One of the most difficult problems plaguing American education is the assessment of teachers. No one denies that teachers ought to be answerable for what they do, but what exactly does that mean? The Oxford American Dictionary defines accountability as: the obligation to give a reckoning or explanation for one's actions.

Does a student have to learn for teaching to have taken place? Historically, teaching has not been defined in this restrictive manner; the teacher was thought to be responsible for the quantity and quality of material covered and the way in which it was presented. However, some definitions of teaching now imply that students must learn in order for teaching to have taken place.

As a teacher who tries my best to keep current on all the latest teaching strategies, I believe that those teachers who do not bother even to pick up an educational journal every once in a while should be kept under close watch. There are many teachers out there who have been teaching for decades and refuse to change their ways even if research has proven that their methods are outdated and ineffective. There is no place in the profession of teaching for these types of individuals. It is time that the American educational system clean house, for the sake of our children.

22. What is the meaning of the word "reckoning" in the third sentence? (Skill 1.1, Average Rigor)

A. Thought
B. Answer
C. Obligation
D. Explanation

23. What is the main idea of the passage? (Skill 2.1, Average Rigor)

A. Teachers should not be answerable for what they do.
B. Teachers who do not do their job should be fired.
C. The author is a good teacher.
D. Assessment of teachers is a serious problem in society today.

24. Is this a valid argument? (Skill 2.4, Easy)

A. Yes
B. No

25. What is the organizational pattern of the second paragraph? (Skill 2.6, Average Rigor)

A. Cause and effect
B. Classification
C. Addition
D. Explanation

ANSWER KEY: READING

1. B
2. C
3. A
4. D
5. C
6. A
7. B
8. B
9. B
10. B
11. A
12. A
13. C
14. A
15. D
16. B
17. C
18. D
19. A
20. D
21. C
22. D
23. D
24. B
25. D

RIGOR TABLE: READING

Easy 20%	Average Rigor 40%	Rigorous 40%
Question # - 6, 8, 13, 20, 24	Question # - 1, 4, 10, 11, 12, 16, 19, 22, 23, 25	Question # - 2, 3, 5, 7, 9, 14, 15, 17, 18, 21

RATIONALES FOR SAMPLE QUESTIONS: READING

Read the passages and answer the questions that follow.

This writer has often been asked to tutor hospitalized children with cystic fibrosis. While undergoing all the precautionary measures to see these children (i.e. scrubbing thoroughly and donning sterilized protective gear- for the child's protection), she has often wondered why their parents subject these children to the pressures of schooling and trying to catch up on what they have missed because of hospitalization, which is a normal part of cystic fibrosis patients' lives. These children undergo so many tortuous treatments a day that it seems cruel to expect them to learn as normal children do, especially with their life expectancies being as short as they are.

1. What is meant by the word "precautionary" in the second sentence? (Skill 1.1, Average Rigor)

A. Careful
B. Protective
C. Medical
D. Sterilizing

The answer is B. The writer uses expressions such as "protective gear" and "child's protection" to emphasize this.

2. What is the main idea of this passage? (Skill 2.1, Rigorous)

A. There is a lot of preparation involved in visiting a, patient of cystic fibrosis.
B. Children with cystic fibrosis are incapable of living normal lives.
C. Certain concessions should be made for children with cystic fibrosis.
D. Children with cystic fibrosis die young.

The answer is C. The author states that she wonders "why parents subject these children to the pressures of schooling" and that "it seems cruel to expect them to learn as normal children do." In making these statements she appears to be expressing the belief that these children should not have to do what "normal" children do. They have enough to deal with – their illness itself.

3. What is the author's tone? (Skill 2.3, Rigorous)

A. Sympathetic
B. Cruel
C. Disbelieving
D. Cheerful

The answer is A. The author states that "it seems cruel to expect them to learn as normal children do," thereby indicating that she feels sorry for them.

4. How is the author so familiar with the procedures used when visiting a child with cystic fibrosis? (Skill 2.3, Average Rigor)

A. She has read about it.
B. She works in a hospital.
C. She is the parent of one.
D. She often tutors them.

The answer is D. The writer states this fact in the opening sentence.

5. What is the author's purpose? (Skill 2.3, Rigorous)

A. To inform
B. To entertain
C. To describe
D. To narrate

The answer is C. The author is simply describing her experience in working with children with cystic fibrosis.

6. Is there evidence of bias in this paragraph? (Skill 2.3, Easy)

A. Yes
B. No

The answer is A. The writer clearly feels sorry for these children and gears her writing in that direction.

7. Does the author present an argument that is valid or invalid concerning the schooling of children with cystic fibrosis? (Skill 2.4, Rigorous)

A. Valid
B. Invalid

The answer is B. Even though to most readers, the writer's argument makes good sense, it is biased and lacks real evidence.

8. The author states that it is "cruel" to expect children with cystic fibrosis to learn as "normal" children do. Is this a fact or an opinion? (Skill 2.5, Easy)

A. Fact
B. Opinion

The answer is B. The fact that she states that it "seems" cruel indicates there is no evidence to support this belief.

9. What type of organizational pattern is the author using? (Skill 2.6, Easy)

A. Classification
B. Explanation
C. Comparison and contrast
D. Cause and effect

The answer is B. The author mentions tutoring children with cystic fibrosis in her opening sentence and goes on to "explain" some of these issues that are involved with her job.

10. What kind of relationship is found within the last sentence which starts with "These children undergo..."and ends with "...as short as they are"? (Skill 2.6, Average Rigor)

A. Addition
B. Explanation
C. Generalization
D. Classification

The answer is B. In mentioning their life expectancies are short, she is explaining by giving one reason why it is cruel to expect them to learn as normal children do.

Disciplinary practices have been found to affect diverse areas of child development such as the acquisition of moral values, obedience to authority, and performance at school. Even though the dictionary has a specific definition of the word "discipline," it is still open to interpretation by people of different cultures.

There are four types of disciplinary styles: assertion of power, withdrawal of love, reasoning, and permissiveness. Assertion of power involves the use of force to discourage unwanted behavior. Withdrawal of love involves making the love of a parent conditional on a child's good behavior. Reasoning involves persuading the child to behave one way rather than another. Permissiveness involves allowing the child to do as he or she pleases and face the consequences of his/her actions.

11. What is the meaning of the word "diverse" in the first sentence? Skill 1.1, Average Rigor)

A. Many
B. Related to children
C. Disciplinary
D. Moral

The answer is A. Any of the other choices would be redundant in this sentence.

12. What is the main idea of this passage? (Skill 2.1, Average Rigor)

A. Different people have different ideas of what discipline is.
B. Permissiveness is the most widely used disciplinary style.
C. Most people agree on their definition of discipline.
D. There are four disciplinary styles.

The answer is A. Choice C is not true; the opposite is stated in the passage. Choice B could be true, but we have no evidence of this. Choice D is just one of the many facts listed in the passage.

13. Name the four types of disciplinary styles. (Skill 2.2, Easy)

A. Reasoning, power assertion, morality, and permissiveness.
B. Morality, reasoning, permissiveness, and withdrawal of love.
C. Withdrawal of love, permissiveness, assertion of power, and reasoning.
D. Permissiveness, morality, reasoning, and power assertion.

The answer is C. This is directly stated in the second paragraph.

14. What does the technique of reasoning involve? (Skill 2.3, Rigorous)

A. Persuading the child to behave in a certain way.
B. Allowing the child to do as he/she pleases.
C. Using force to discourage unwanted behavior.
D. Making love conditional on good behavior.

The answer is A. This fact is directly stated in the second paragraph.

15. What is the author's purpose in writing this? (Skill 2.3, Rigorous)

A. To describe
B. To narrate
C. To entertain
D. To inform

The answer is D. The author is providing the reader with information about disciplinary practices.

16. Is this passage biased? (Skill 2.3, Average Rigor)

A. Yes
B. No

The answer is B. If the reader were so inclined, he could research discipline and find this information.

17. What is the author's tone? (Skill 2.3, Rigorous)

A. Disbelieving
B. Angry
C. Informative
D. Optimistic

The answer is C. The author appears to simply be stating the facts.

18. From reading this passage we can conclude that (Skill 2.3, Rigorous)

A. The author is a teacher.
B. The author has many children.
C. The author has written a book about discipline.
D. The author has done a lot of research on discipline.

The answer is D. Given all the facts mentioned in the passage, this is the only inference one can make.

19. The author states that "assertion of power involves the use of force to discourage unwanted behavior." Is this a fact or an opinion? (Skill 2.5, Average Rigor)

A. Fact
B. Opinion

The answer is A. The author appears to have done extensive research on this subject.

20. What organizational structure is used in the first sentence of the second paragraph? (Skill 2.6, Easy)

A. Addition
B. Explanation
C. Definition
D. Simple listing

The answer is D. The author simply states the types of disciplinary styles.

21. What is the overall organizational pattern of this passage? (Skill 2.6, Rigorous)

A. Generalization
B. Cause and effect
C. Addition
D. Summary

The answer is C. The author has taken a subject, in this case discipline, and developed it point by point.

One of the most difficult problems plaguing American education is the assessment of teachers. No one denies that teachers ought to be answerable for what they do, but what exactly does that mean? The Oxford American Dictionary defines accountability as: the obligation to give a reckoning or explanation for one's actions.

Does a student have to learn for teaching to have taken place? Historically, teaching has not been defined in this restrictive manner; the teacher was thought to be responsible for the quantity and quality of material covered and the way in which it was presented. However, some definitions of teaching now imply that students must learn in order for teaching to have taken place.

As a teacher who tries my best to keep current on all the latest teaching strategies, I believe that those teachers who do not bother even to pick up an educational journal every once in a while should be kept under close watch. There are many teachers out there who have been teaching for decades and refuse to change their ways even if research has proven that their methods are outdated and ineffective. There is no place in the profession of teaching for these types of individuals. It is time that the American educational system clean house, for the sake of our children.

22. What is the meaning of the word "reckoning" in the third sentence? (Skill 1.1, Average Rigor)

A. Thought
B. Answer
C. Obligation
D. Explanation

The answer is D. The meaning of this word is directly stated in the same sentence.

23. What is the main idea of the passage? (Skill 2.1, Average Rigor)

A. Teachers should not be answerable for what they do.
B. Teachers who do not do their job should be fired.
C. The author is a good teacher.
D. Assessment of teachers is a serious problem in society today.

The answer is D. Most of the passage is dedicated to elaborating on why teacher assessment is such a problem.

24. Is this a valid argument? (Skill 2.4, Easy)

A. Yes
B. No

The answer is B. In the third paragraph, the author appears to be resentful of lazy teachers.

25. What is the organizational pattern of the second paragraph? (Skill 2.6, Average Rigor)

A. Cause and effect
B. Classification
C. Addition
D. Explanation

The answer is D. The author goes on to further explain what she meant by"...what exactly does that mean?" in the first paragraph.

COMPETENCY 4.0 UNDERSTAND PARTS OF SPEECH, PARTS OF SENTENCES, AND PROPER USAGE IN STANDARD AMERICAN ENGLISH

Skill 4.1 Recognize parts of speech (nouns, pronouns, verbs, adjectives, adverbs, prepositions, conjunctions, interjections)

The eight parts of speech form the syntactical framework on our language. While the study of grammar can be detailed, let's review some of the basics.

- Noun—names a person, place, or thing
- Pronoun—takes the place of one or more noun
- Verb—expresses action or state of being
- Adjective—describes, or modifies, a noun or a pronoun
- Adverb—modifies a verb, an adjective, or another adverb
- Conjunction—is a connecting word
- Preposition—relates a noun or a pronoun to another word in a sentence
- Interjection—expresses emotions

Nouns

A **noun** names a person, place, or thing/idea. A common noun names any person, place, or thing/idea; a proper noun names a particular person, place, thing/idea and will be capitalized.

	Person	Place	Thing/Idea	Idea
Common Noun	Actor	museum	ship	bravery
Proper Noun	Meryl Streep	The Smithsonian	*Titanic*	

Concentration in this section will be on spelling plurals and possessives. The multiplicity and complexity of spelling rules based on phonics, letter doubling, and exceptions to rules—not mastered by adulthood—should be replaced by a good dictionary. As spelling mastery is also difficult for adolescents, our recommendation is the same. Learning the use of a dictionary and thesaurus will be a more rewarding use of time.

Plural Nouns

The multiplicity and complexity of spelling rules based on phonics, letter doubling, and exceptions to rules—not mastered by adulthood—should be replaced by a good dictionary. As spelling mastery is also difficult for adolescents, our recommendation is the same. Learning the use of a dictionary and thesaurus will be a more rewarding use of time.

Most plurals of nouns that end in hard consonants or hard consonant sounds followed by a silent *e* are made by adding *s.* Some words ending in vowels only add *s.*

fingers, numerals, banks, bugs, riots, homes, gates, radios, bananas

Nouns that end in soft consonant sounds *s, j, x, z, ch,* and *sh,* add *es.* Some nouns ending in *o* add *es.*

dresses, waxes, churches, brushes, tomatoes

Nouns ending in *y* preceded by a vowel just add *s.*

boys, alleys

Nouns ending in *y* preceded by a consonant change the *y* to *i* and add *es.*

babies, corollaries, frugalities, poppies

Some nouns' plurals are formed irregularly or remain the same.
sheep, deer, children, leaves, oxen

Some nouns derived from foreign words, especially Latin, may make their plurals in two different ways - one of them Anglicized. Sometimes, the meanings are the same; other times, the two plurals are used in slightly different contexts. It is always wise to consult the dictionary.

appendices, appendixes
indexes, indices
criterion, criteria
crisis, crises

Make the plurals of closed (solid) compound words in the usual way except for words ending in *ful* which make their plurals on the root word.

timelines, hairpins

Make the plurals of open or hyphenated compounds by adding the change in inflection to the word that change in number.

fathers-in-law, courts-martial, masters of art, doctors of medicine

Make the plurals of letters, numbers, and abbreviations by adding *s.*

fives and tens, IBMs, 1990s, *p*s and *q*s (Note that letters are italicized.)

Possessive Nouns

Make the possessives of singular nouns by adding an apostrophe followed by the letter *s ('s).*

baby's bottle, father's job, elephant's eye, teacher's desk, sympathizer's protests, week's postponement

Make the possessive of singular nouns ending in *s* by adding either an apostrophe or an *('s)* depending upon common usage or sound. When making the possessive causes difficulty, use a prepositional phrase instead. Even with the sibilant ending, with a few exceptions, it is advisable to use the *('s)* construction.

dress's color, species' characteristics or characteristics of the species, James' hat or James's hat, Delores's shirt. Make the possessive of plural nouns ending in *s* by adding the apostrophe after the *s;* horses' coats, jockeys' times, four days' time

Make possessives of plural nouns that do not end in *s* the same as singular nouns by adding *'s.*

children's shoes, deer's antlers, cattle's horns

Make possessives of compound nouns by adding the inflection at the end of the word or phrase.

the mayor of Los Angeles' campaign, the mailman's new truck, the mailmen's new trucks, my father-in-law's first wife, the keepsakes' values, several daughters-in-law's husbands

Note: Because a gerund functions as a noun, any noun preceding it and operating as a possessive adjective must reflect the necessary inflection. However, if the gerundive following the noun is a participle, no inflection is added.

The general was perturbed by the private's sleeping on duty. (The word *sleeping* is a gerund, the object of the preposition *by.)*
but
The general was perturbed to see the private sleeping on duty. (The word *sleeping* is a participle modifying private.)

Rules for Clearly Identifying Pronoun Reference

Make sure that the antecedent reference is clear and cannot refer to something else. A "distant relative" is a relative pronoun or a relative clause that has been placed too far away from the antecedent to which it refers. It is a common error to place a verb between the relative pronoun and its antecedent.

Error: Return the books to the library that are overdue.

Problem: The relative clause "that are overdue" refers to the "books" and should be placed immediately after the antecedent.

Correction: *Return the books that are overdue to the library.*
or
Return the overdue books to the library.

A pronoun should not refer to adjectives or possessive nouns. Adjectives, nouns or possessive pronouns should not be used as antecedents. This will create ambiguity in sentences.

Error: In Todd's letter he told his mom he'd broken the priceless vase.

Problem: In this sentence the pronoun "he" seems to refer to the noun phrase "Todd's letter" though it was probably meant to refer to the possessive noun "Todd's."

Correction: *In his letter, Todd told his mom that he had broken the priceless vase.*

A pronoun should not refer to an implied idea. A pronoun must refer to a specific antecedent rather than an implied antecedent. When an antecedent is not stated specifically, the reader has to guess or assume the meaning of a sentence. Pronouns that do not have antecedents are called expletives. "It" and "there" are the most common expletives, though other pronouns can also become expletives as well. In informal conversation, expletives allow for casual presentation of ideas without supporting evidence. However, in more formal writing, it is best to be more precise.

Error: She said that it is important to floss every day.

Problem: The pronoun "it" refers to an implied idea.

Correction: *She said that flossing every day is important.*

Error: They returned the book because there were missing pages.

Problem: The pronouns "they" and "there" do not refer to the antecedent.

Correction: *The customer returned the book with missing pages.*

Using Who, That, and Which

Who, whom and **whose** refer to human beings and can either introduce essential or nonessential clauses. **That** refers to things other than humans and is used to introduce essential clauses. **Which** refers to things other than humans and is used to introduce nonessential clauses.

Error: The doctor that performed the surgery said the man would be fully recovered.

Problem: Since the relative pronoun is referring to a human, who should be used.

Correction: *The doctor who performed the surgery said the man would be fully recovered.*

Error: That ice cream cone that you just ate looked really delicious.

Problem: That has already been used so you must use *which* to introduce the next clause, whether it is essential or nonessential.

Correction: *That ice cream cone, which you just ate, looked really delicious.*

Proper Case Forms

Pronouns, unlike nouns, change case forms. Pronouns must be in the subjective, objective, or possessive form according to their function in the sentence.

Subjective (Nominative)			**Possessive**		**Objective**	
	Singular	Plural	Singular	Plural	Singular	Plural
1st person	I	we	my	our	me	us
2nd person	you	you	your	your	you	you
3rd person	he she it	they	his her its	their	him her it	them

Relative Pronouns

Who Subjective/Nominative
Whom Objective
Whose Possessive

Error: Tom and me have reserved seats for next week's baseball game.

Problem: The pronoun me is the subject of the verb have reserved and should be in the subjective form.

Correction: *Tom and I have reserved seats for next week's baseball game.*

Error: Who's coat is this?

Problem: The interrogative possessive pronoun is whose; who's is the contraction for who is.

Correction: *Whose coat is this?*

Error: The voters will choose the candidate whom has the best qualifications for the job.

Problem: The case of the relative pronoun *who* or *whom* is determined by the pronoun's function in the clause in which it appears. The word *who* is in the subjective case, and whom is in the objective. Analyze how the pronoun is being used within the sentence.

Correction: *The voters will choose the candidate who has the best qualifications for the job.*

Practice Exercise: Pronoun Case

Choose the option that corrects an error in the underlined portion(s). If no error exists, choose "No change is necessary."

1. Even though Sheila and he had planned to be alone at the diner, they were joined by three friends of their's instead.

   A. him
   B. him and her
   C. theirs
   D. No change is necessary.

2. Uncle Walter promised to give his car to whomever will guarantee to drive it safely.

   A. whom
   B. whoever
   C. them
   D. No change is necessary.

3. Eddie and him gently laid the body on the ground next to the sign.

   A. he
   B. them
   C. it
   D. No change is necessary.

4. Mary, who is competing in the chess tournament, is a better player than me.

   A. whose
   B. whom
   C. I
   D. No change is necessary.

5. We, ourselves, have decided not to buy property in that development; however, our friends have already bought themselves some land.

   A. We, ourself,
   B. their selves
   C. their self
   D. No change is necessary.

Answer Key: Practice Exercise for Pronoun Case

1. The correct answer is C. The possessive pronoun *theirs* doesn't need an apostrophe. Option A is incorrect because the subjective pronoun *he* is needed in this sentence. Option B is incorrect because the subjective pronoun *they*, not the objective pronouns *him* and *her*, is needed.

2. The correct answer is B. The subjective case *whoever*—not the objective case *whomever*—is the subject of the relative clause *whoever will guarantee to drive it safely*. Option A is incorrect because *whom* is an objective pronoun. Option C is incorrect because *car* is singular and takes the pronoun *it*.

3. The correct answer is A. The subjective pronoun *he* is needed as the subject of the verb *laid*. Option B is incorrect because *them* is vague; the noun *body* is needed to clarify *it*. Option C is incorrect because *it* is vague, and the noun *sign* is necessary for clarification.

4. The correct answer is C. The subjective pronoun *I* is needed because the comparison is understood. Option A incorrectly uses the possessive *whose*. Option B is incorrect because the subjective pronoun *who*, and not the objective *whom*, is needed.

5. The correct answer is B. The reflexive pronoun *themselves* refers to the plural *friends*. Option A is incorrect because the plural *we* requires the reflexive *ourselves*. Option C is incorrect because the possessive pronoun *their* is never joined with either *self* or *selves*.

Verbs

A verb expresses action or state of being. Most verbs show time (tense) by an inflectional ending to the word. Other irregular verbs take completely different forms.

Both regular and irregular verbs must appear in their standard forms for each tense. Note: the *ed* or *d* ending is added to regular verbs in the past tense and for past participles.

Infinitive	Past Tense	Past Participle
bake	baked	baked

Irregular Verb Forms

Infinitive	Past Tense	Past Participle
be	was, were	been
become	became	become
break	broke	broken
bring	brought	brought
choose	chose	chosen
come	came	come
do	did	done
draw	drew	drawn
eat	ate	eaten
fall	fell	fallen
forget	forgot	forgotten
freeze	froze	frozen
give	gave	given
go	went	gone
grow	grew	grown
have/has	had	had
hide	hid	hidden
know	knew	known
lay	laid	laid
lie	lay	lain
ride	rode	ridden
rise	rose	risen
run	ran	run
see	saw	seen
steal	stole	stolen
take	took	taken
tell	told	told
throw	threw	thrown
wear	wore	worn
write	wrote	written

Error: She should have went to her doctor's appointment at the scheduled time.

Problem: The past participle of the verb to go is gone. Went expresses the simple past tense.

Correction: *She should have gone to her doctor's appointment at the scheduled time.*

Error: My train is suppose to arrive before two o'clock.

Problem: The verb following *train* is a present tense passive construction which requires the present tense verb *to be* and the past participle.

Correction: *My train is supposed to arrive before two o'clock.*

Error: Linda should of known that the car wouldn't start after leaving it out in the cold all night.

Problem: *Should of* is a nonstandard expression. *Of* is not a verb.

Correction: *Linda should have known that the car wouldn't start after leaving it out in the cold all night.*

Practice Exercise: Standard Verb Forms

Choose the option that corrects an error in the underlined portion(s). If no error exists, choose "No change is necessary."

1. My professor had knew all along that we would pass his course.

   A. know
   B. had known
   C. knowing
   D. No change is necessary.

2. Kevin was asked to erase the vulgar words he had wrote.

   A. writes
   B. has write
   C. had written
   D. No change is necessary.

3. Melanie had forget to tell her parents that she left the cat in the closet.

   A. had forgotten
   B. forgot
   C. forget
   D. No change is necessary.

4. Craig always leave the house a mess when his parents aren't there.

   A. left
   B. leaves
   C. leaving
   D. No change is necessary.

5. The store manager accused Kathy of having stole more than five hundred dollars from the safe.

   A. has stolen
   B. having stolen
   C. stole
   D. No change is necessary.

Answer Key: Practice Exercise for Standard Verb Forms

1. Option B is correct because the past participle needs the helping verb had. Option A is incorrect because it is in the infinitive tense. Option C incorrectly uses the present participle.

2. Option C is correct because the past participle follows the helping verb had. Option A uses the verb in the present tense. Option B is an incorrect use of the verb.

3. Option A is correct because the past participle uses the helping verb had. Option B uses the wrong form of the verb. Option C uses the wrong form of the verb.

4. Option B correctly uses the past tense of the verb. Option A uses the verb in an incorrect way. Option C uses the verb without a helping verb like is.

5. Option B is correct because it is the past participle. Option A and C use the verb incorrectly.

Adjectives and Adverbs

Adjectives are words that modify or describe nouns or pronouns. Adjectives usually precede the words they modify, but not always; for example, an adjective occurs after a linking verb. Adjectives answer what kind, how many, or which one.

Adverbs are words that modify verbs, adjectives, or other adverbs. They cannot modify nouns. Adverbs answer such questions as how, why, when, where, how much, or how often something is done. Many adverbs are formed by adding *ly*.

Error: The birthday cake tasted sweetly.

Problem: *Tasted* is a linking verb; the modifier that follows should be an adjective, not an adverb.

Correction: *The birthday cake tasted sweet.*

Check out this
Guide to Grammar and Writing
http://grammar.ccc.commnet.edu/grammar/

Error: You have done good with this project.

Problem: *Good* is an adjective and cannot be used to modify a verb phrase such as have done.

Correction: *You have done well with this project.*

Error: The coach was positive happy about the team's chance of winning.

Problem: The adjective *positive* cannot be used to modify another adjective, *happy*. An adverb is needed instead.

Correction: *The coach was positively happy about the team's chance of winning.*

Error: The fireman acted quick and brave to save the child from the burning building.

Problem: *Quick and brave* are adjectives and cannot be used to describe a verb. Adverbs are needed instead.

Correction: *The fireman acted quickly and bravely to save the child from the burning building.*

Practice Exercise: Adjectives and Adverbs

Choose the option that corrects an error in the underlined portion(s). If no error exists, choose "No change is necessary."

1. Moving quick throughout the house, the burglar removed several priceless antiques before carelessly dropping his wallet.

   A. quickly
   B. remove
   C. careless
   D. No change is necessary.

2. The car crashed loudly into the retaining wall before spinning wildly on the sidewalk.

   A. crashes
   B. loudly
   C. wild
   D. No change is necessary.

3. The airplane landed safe on the runway after nearly colliding with a helicopter.

   A. land
   B. safely
   C. near
   D. No change is necessary.

4. The horribly bad special effects in the movie disappointed us great.

   A. horrible
   B. badly
   C. greatly
   D. No change is necessary.

5. The man promised to faithfully obey the rules of the social club.

   A. faithful
   B. faithfulness
   C. faith
   D. No change is necessary.

Answer Key: Practice Exercise for Adjectives and Adverbs

1. Option A is correct. The adverb *quickly* is needed to modify *moving*. Option B is incorrect because it uses the wrong form of the verb. Option C is incorrect because the adverb *carelessly* is needed before the verb *dropping,* not the adjective *careless*.

2. Option D is correct. The sentence is correct as it is written. Adverbs *loudly* and *wildly* are needed to modify *crashed* and *spinning*. Option A incorrectly uses the verb *crashes* instead of the participle *crashing*, which acts as an adjective.

3. Option B is correct. The adverb *safely* is needed to modify the verb *landed.* Option A is incorrect because *land* is a noun. Option C is incorrect because *near* is an adjective, not an adverb.

4. Option C is correct. The adverb *greatly* is needed to modify the verb *disappointed.* Option A is incorrect because *horrible* is an adjective, not an adverb. Option B is incorrect because *bad* needs to modify the adverb *horribly*.

5. Option D is correct. The adverb *faithfully* is the correct modifier of the verb *promised.* Option A is an adjective used to modify nouns. Neither Option B nor Option C, which are both nouns, is a modifier.

Conjunctions

A conjunction connects words, phrases, or clauses. It acts as a signal, indicating when a thought is added, contrasted, or altered.

Meet the FANBOYS!

For, And, Nor, But, Or, Yet, So

These are **coordinating conjunctions** that join similar elements.

Strong and tall (adjectives)
Easily and quickly (adverbs)
Of the people, by the people, for the people (prepositional phrases)
We disagreed, but we reached a compromise. (sentences)

Subordinating conjunctions connect clauses (subject-verb combinations) in a sentence. They signal that the clause is subordinate and cannot stand alone.

Subordinating Conjunctions			
after	because	though	whenever
although	before	till	where
as	if	unless	whereas
as if	since	until	wherever
as though	than	when	while

I will be grateful *if you will work on this project with me.*
Because I am running late, you will need to cover for me.

Prepositions

A preposition relates a noun or a pronoun to another word in a sentence. Below is a partial list.

about	above	according to	across	after	against
along	along with	among	apart from	around	as/as for
at	because of	before	behind	below	beneath
beside	between	beyond	by	by means of	concerning
despite	down	during	except	except for	excepting
for	from	in	in addition to	in back of	in case of
in front of	in place of	inside	in spite of	instead of	into
like	near	next	of	off	on
onto	on top of	out/out of	outside	over	past
regarding	round	since	through	throughout	till
to	toward	under	underneath	unlike	until
up/upon	up to	with	within	without	

Guidelines

- Include necessary prepositions.

  I graduated from high school. (not *I graduated high school.*)

- Omit unnecessary prepositions

  Both printers work well. (Not *Both of the printers* work well.)
  Where are the printers? (Not *Where are the printers at?*)

- Avoid the overuse of prepositions.

  We have received your application for credit at our branch in the Fresno area.
  We have received your Fresno credit application.

Interjections

An **interjection** is a word or group of words that express emotion, surprise, or disbelief. It has no grammatical connection to other words in a sentence.

Some Common Interjections			
aha	great	my	ouch
alas	ha	no	well
gee	hey	oh	wow
good grief	hooray	oops	yes

Guidelines

- When an interjection expresses strong emotion, it usually stands alone; it begins with a capital letter and ends with an exclamation point.

  Ouch! That paper cut really hurts.
  Good grief! My favorite store has closed.

- When an interjection expresses mild feeling, it is written as part of the sentence and is set off with commas.

  Yes, we will comply with your request.

Skill 4.2 Recognize parts of a sentence (e.g., subject, verb, complement)

Sentence structure

Recognize simple, compound, complex, and compound-complex sentences. Use dependent (subordinate) and independent clauses correctly to create these sentence structures.

Simple—Consists of one independent clause

Joyce wrote a letter.

Compound—Consists of two or more independent clauses. The two clauses are usually connected by a coordinating conjunction (and, but, or, nor, for, so, yet). Compound sentences are sometimes connected by semicolons.

Joyce wrote a letter, and Dot drew a picture.

Complex—Consists of an independent clause plus one or more dependent clauses. The dependent clause may precede the independent clause or follow it.

While Joyce wrote a letter, Dot drew a picture.

Compound/Complex—Consists of one or more dependent clauses plus two or more independent clauses .

When Mother asked the girls to demonstrate their new-found skills, Joyce wrote a letter, and Dot drew a picture.

Note: Do **not** confuse compound sentence elements with compound sentences.

Simple sentence with compound subject

Joyce and Dot wrote letters.
The girl in row three and the boy next to her were passing notes across the aisle.

Simple sentence with compound predicate

Joyce wrote letters and drew pictures.
The captain of the high school debate team graduated with honors and studied broadcast journalism in college.

Simple sentence with compound object of preposition

Coleen graded the students' essays for style and mechanical accuracy.

Types of Clauses

Clauses are connected word groups that are composed of *at least* one subject and one verb. (A subject is the doer of an action or the element that is being joined. A verb conveys either the action or the link.)

Students are waiting for the start of the assembly.
Subject Verb

At the end of the play, students wait for the curtain to come down.
Subject Verb

Clauses can be independent or dependent. Independent clauses can stand alone or can be joined to other clauses.

Comma and coordinating conjunction

Independent clause	, for	Independent clause
	, and	Independent clause
	, nor	Independent clause
	, but	Independent clause
	, or	Independent clause
	, yet	Independent clause
	, so	Independent clause

Semicolon

Independent clause	;	Independent clause

Subordinating conjunction, dependent clause, and comma

Dependent clause	,	Independent clause

Independent clause followed by a subordinating conjunction that introduces a dependent clause

Independent clause	Dependent clause

Dependent clauses, by definition, contain at least one subject and one verb. However, they cannot stand alone as a complete sentence. They are structurally dependent on the main clause.

There are two types of dependent clauses: (1) those with a subordinating conjunction, and (2) those with a relative pronoun.

Sample subordinating conjunctions

Although   When   If   Unless   Because

Unless a cure is discovered, many more people will die of the disease.
Dependent clause + Independent clause

Sample relative pronouns

Who   Whom   Which   That

The White House has an official website, which contains press releases, news updates, and biographies of the President and Vice-President.
(Independent clause + relative pronoun + relative dependent clause)

Skill 4.3 Recognize the standard use of verbs (e.g., subject-verb agreement, verb tense)

Agreement Between Subject and Verb

A verb must correspond in the singular or plural form with the simple subject; it is not affected by any interfering elements. Note: A simple subject is never found in a prepositional phrase (a phrase beginning with a word such as of, by, over, through, until).

Present Tense Verb Form

	Singular	Plural
1st person (talking about oneself)	I do	We do
2nd person (talking to another)	You do	You do
3rd person (talking about someone or something)	He She does It	They do

Error: Sally, as well as her sister, plan to go into nursing.

Problem: The subject in the sentence is *Sally* alone, not the word *sister*. Therefore, the verb must be singular.

Correction: *Sally, as well as her sister, plans to go into nursing.*

Error: There has been many car accidents lately on that street.

Problem: The subject *accidents* in this sentence is plural; the verb must be plural also—even though it comes before the subject.

Correction: *There have been many car accidents lately on that street.*

Error: Everyone of us have a reason to attend the school musical.

Problem: The simple subject is the word *everyone*, not the *us* in the prepositional phrase. Therefore, the verb must be singular also.

Correction: *Everyone of us has a reason to attend the school musical.*

Error: Either the police captain or his officers is going to the convention.

Problem: In either/or and neither/nor constructions, the verb agrees with the subject closer to it.

Correction: *Either the police captain or his officers are going to the convention.*

Practice Exercise: Subject-Verb Agreement

Choose the option that corrects an error in the underlined portion(s). If no error exists, choose "No change is necessary."

1. Every year, the store stays open late, when shoppers desperately try to purchase Christmas presents as they prepare for the holiday.

   A. stay
   B. tries
   C. prepared
   D. No change is necessary.

2. Paul McCartney, together with George Harrison and Ringo Starr, sing classic Beatles songs on a special greatest-hits CD.

   A. singing
   B. sings
   C. sung
   D. No change is necessary.

3. My friend's cocker spaniel, while chasing cats across the street, always manages to knock over the trash cans.

   A. chased
   B. manage
   C. knocks
   D. No change is necessary.

4. Some of the ice on the driveway have melted.

   A. having melted
   B. has melted
   C. has melt.
   D. No change is necessary.

5. Neither the criminal forensics expert nor the DNA blood evidence provided enough support for that verdict.

   A. provides
   B. were providing
   C. are providing
   D. No change is necessary.

Answer Key: Practice Exercise for Subject-Verb Agreement

1. Option D is correct because *store* is third person singular and requires the third person singular verbs *stays*. Option B is incorrect because the plural noun *shoppers* requires a plural verb *try*. In Option C, there is no reason to shift to the past tense *prepared*.

2. Option B is correct because the subject, *Paul McCartney,* is singular and requires the singular verb *sings*. Option A is incorrect because the present participle *singing* does not stand alone as a verb. Option C is incorrect because the past participle *sung* alone cannot function as the verb in this sentence.

3. Option D is the correct answer because the subject *cocker spaniel* is singular and requires the singular verb *manages*. Options A, B, and C do not work structurally with the sentence.

4. Option B is correct. The subject of the sentence is *some*, which requires a third person singular verb, *has melted*. Option A incorrectly uses the present participle *having*, which does not act as a helping verb. Option C does not work structurally with the sentence.

5. Option A is correct. In Option A, the singular subject *evidence* is closer to the verb and thus requires the singular in the neither/nor construction. Both Options B and C are plural forms with the helping verb and the present participle.

Verb tenses must refer to the same time period consistently, unless a change in time is required.

Error: Despite the increased amount of students in the school this year, overall attendance is higher last year at the sporting events.

Problem: The verb *is* represents an inconsistent shift to the present tense when the action refers to a past occurrence.

Correction: *Despite the increased amount of students in the school this year, overall attendance was higher last year at sporting events.*

Error: My friend Lou, who just competed in the marathon, ran since he was twelve years old.

Problem: Because Lou continues to run, the present perfect tense is needed.

Correction: *My friend Lou, who just competed in the marathon, has run since he was twelve years old.*

Error: The Mayor congratulated Wallace Mangham, who renovates the city hall last year.

Problem: Although the speaker is talking in the present, the action of renovating the city hall was in the past.

Correction: *The Mayor congratulated Wallace Mangham, who renovated the city hall last year.*

Practice Exercise: Shifts in Tense

Choose the option that corrects an error in the underlined portion(s). If no error exists, choose "No change is necessary."

1. After we washed the fruit that had growing in the garden, we knew there was a store that would buy them.

   A. washing
   B. grown
   C. is
   D. No change is necessary.

2. The tourists used to visit the Atlantic City boardwalk whenever they vacationed during the summer. Unfortunately, their numbers have diminished every year.

   A. use
   B. vacation
   C. diminish
   D. No change is necessary.

3. When the temperature drops to below thirty-two degrees Fahrenheit, the water on the lake freezes, which allowed children to skate across it.

   A. dropped
   B. froze
   C. allows
   D. No change is necessary.

4. The artists were hired to create a monument that would pay tribute to the men who were killed in World War Two.

   A. hiring
   B. created
   C. killing
   D. No change is necessary.

5. Emergency medical personnel rushed to the scene of the shooting, where many injured people waiting for treatment.

   A. wait
   B. waited
   C. waits
   D. No change is necessary.

Answer Key: Practice Exercise for Shifts in Tense

1. Option B is correct. The past participle *grown* is needed instead of *growing* which is the progressive tense. Option A is incorrect because the past participle *washed* takes the *ed*. Option C incorrectly replaces the past participle *was* with the present tense *is*.

2. Option D is correct. Option A is incorrect because *use* is the present tense. Option B incorrectly uses the noun *vacation*. Option C incorrectly uses the present tense *diminish* instead of the past tense *diminished*.

3. Option C is correct. The present tense *allows* is necessary in the context of the sentence. Option A is incorrect because *dropped* is a past participle. Option B is incorrect because *froze* is also a past participle.

4. Option D is correct. In Option A is incorrect because *hiring* is the present tense. In Option B is incorrect because *created* is a past participle. In Option C, *killing*, doesn't fit into the context of the sentence.

5. Option B is correct. In Option B, *waited*, corresponds with the past tense *rushed*. In Option A, *wait*, is incorrect because it is present tense. In Option C, *waits*, is incorrect because the noun *people* is plural and requires the singular form of the verb.

Skill 4.4 Recognize the standard use of pronouns (e.g., pronoun-antecedent agreement)

Agreements Between Pronoun and Antecedent

A pronoun must correspond to its antecedent in number (singular or plural), person (first, second or third person) and gender (male, female or neutral). A pronoun must refer clearly to a single word, not to a complete idea.

A **pronoun shift** is a grammatical error in which the author starts a sentence, paragraph, or section of a paper using one particular type of pronoun and then suddenly shifts to another. This often confuses the reader.

Error: A teacher should treat all their students fairly.

Problem: Since *A teacher* is singular, the pronoun referring to it must also be singular. Otherwise, the noun has to be made plural.

Correction: *Teachers should treat all their students fairly.*

Error: When an actor is rehearsing for a play, it often helps if you can memorize the lines in advance.

Problem: *Actor* is a third-person word; that is, the writer is talking about the subject. The pronoun *you* is in the second person, which means the writer is talking to the subject.

Correction: *When actors are rehearsing for plays, it helps if they can memorize the lines in advance.*

Error: The workers in the factory were upset when his or her paychecks didn't arrive on time.

Problem: *Workers* is a plural form, while *his or her* refers to one person.

Correction: *The workers in the factory were upset when their paychecks didn't arrive on time.*

Error: The charity auction was highly successful, which pleased everyone.

Problem: In this sentence the pronoun *which* refers to the idea of the auction's success. In fact, *which* has no antecedent in the sentence; the word success is not stated.

Correction: *Everyone was pleased at the success of the auction.*

Error: Lana told Melanie that she would like aerobics.

Problem: The person that she refers to is unclear; it could be either Lana or Melanie.

Correction: *Lana said that Melanie would like aerobics.*

or

Lana told Melanie that she, Melanie, would like aerobics.

Error: I dislike accounting, even though my brother is one.

Problem: A person's occupation is not the same as a field, and the pronoun *one* is thus incorrect. Note that the word *accountant* is not used in the sentence, so *one* has no antecedent.

Correction: *I dislike accounting, even though my brother is an accountant.*

PRACTICE EXERCISE – PRONOUN/ANTECEDENT AGREEMENT

Choose the option that corrects an error in the underlined portion(s). If no error exists, choose "No change is necessary."

1. You can get to Martha's Vineyard by driving from Boston to Woods Hole. Once there, you can travel over on a ship, but you may find traveling by airplane to be an exciting experience.

   A. they
   B. visitors
   C. it
   D. No change is necessary.

2. Both the city leader and the journalist are worried about the new interstate; she fears the new roadway will destroy precious farmland.

   A. journalist herself
   B. they fear
   C. it
   D. No change is necessary.

3. When hunters are looking for deer in the woods, you must remain quiet for long periods of time.

   A. they
   B. it
   C. we
   D. No change is necessary.

4. Florida's strong economy is based on the importance of the citrus industry. Producing orange juice for most of the country.

   A. They produce
   B. Who produce
   C. Farmers there produce
   D. No change is necessary.

5. Dr. Kennedy told Paul Elliot, his assistant, that he would have to finish grading the tests before going home, no matter how long it took.

   A. their
   B. he, Paul
   C. they
   D. No change is necessary.

Answer Key: Practice Exercise for Pronoun Agreement

1. Option D is correct. Pronouns must be consistent. As *you* is used throughout the sentence, the shift to *visitors* is incorrect. Option A, *They*, is vague and unclear. Option C, *it*, is also unclear.

2. Option B is correct. The plural pronoun *they* is necessary to agree with the two nouns *leader* and *journalist*. There is no need for the reflexive pronoun *herself* in Option A. Option C, *it*, is vague.

3. Option A is correct. The shift to *you* is unnecessary. The plural pronoun *they* is necessary to agree with the noun *hunters*. The word *we* in Option C is vague; the reader does not know who the word *we* might refer to. Option B, *it*, has no antecedent.

4. Option C is correct. The noun *farmers* is needed for clarification because *producing* is vague. Option A is incorrect because *they produce* is vague. Option B is incorrect because *who* has no antecedent and creates a fragment.

5. Option B is correct. The repetition of the name *Paul* is necessary to clarify who the pronoun *he* is referring to. (It could be Dr. Kennedy.) Option A is incorrect because the singular pronoun *his* is needed, not the plural pronoun *their*. Option C is incorrect because the pronoun *it* refers to the plural noun *tests*.

Skill 4.5 Recognize the standard use of modifiers (e.g., adjectives, adverbs)

Particular phrases that are not placed near the one word they modify often result in misplaced **modifiers**. Particular phrases that do not relate to the subject being modified result in dangling modifiers.

Error: Weighing the options carefully, a decision was made regarding the punishment of the convicted murderer.

Problem: Who is weighing the options? No one capable of weighing is named in the sentence; thus, the participle phrase *weighing the options carefully* dangles. This problem can be corrected by adding a subject of the sentence capable of doing the action.

Correction: *Weighing the options carefully, the judge made a decision regarding the punishment of the convicted murderer.*

Error: Returning to my favorite watering hole, brought back many fond memories.

Problem: The person who returned is never indicated, and the participle phrase dangles. This problem can be corrected by creating a dependent clause from the modifying phrase.

Correction: *When I returned to my favorite watering hole, many fond memories came back to me.*

Error: Recovered from the five-mile hike, the obstacle course was a piece of cake for the Boy Scout troop.

Problem: The obstacle course is not recovered from the five-mile hike, so the modifying phrase must be placed closer to the word, *troop*, that it modifies.

Correction: *The obstacle course was a piece of cake for the Boy Scout troop, which had just recovered from a five-mile hike.*

Practice Exercise: Misplaced and Dangling Modifiers

Choose the sentence that expresses the thought most clearly and effectively and that has no error in structure.

1. A. Attempting to remove the dog from the well, the paramedic tripped and fell in also.

   B. As the paramedic attempted to remove the dog from the well, he tripped and fell in also.

   C. The paramedic tripped and fell in also attempting to remove the dog from the well.

2. A. To save the wounded child, a powerful explosion ripped through the operating room as the doctors worked.

   B. In the operating room, as the wounded child was being saved, a powerful explosion ripped through.

   C. To save the wounded child, the doctors worked as an explosion ripped through the operating room.

3. A. One hot July morning, a herd of giraffes screamed wildly in the jungle next to the wildlife habitat.

   B. One hot July morning, a herd of giraffes screamed in the jungle wildly next to the wildlife habitat.

   C. One hot July morning, a herd of giraffes screamed in the jungle next to the wildlife habitat, wildly.

4. A. Looking through the file cabinets in the office, the photographs of the crime scene revealed a new suspect in the investigation.

   B. Looking through the file cabinets in the office, the detective discovered photographs of the crime scene which revealed a new suspect in the investigation.

   C. A new suspect in the investigation was revealed in photographs of the crime scene that were discovered while looking through the file cabinets in the office.

Answer Key: Practice Exercise for Misplaced and Dangling Modifiers

1. Option B corrects the dangling participle *attempting to remove the dog from the well* by creating a dependent clause introducing the main clause. In Option A, the introductory participle phrase *Attempting...well* does not refer to a paramedic, the subject of the main clause. The word also in Option C incorrectly implies that the paramedic was doing something besides trying to remove the dog.

2. Option C corrects the dangling modifier *to save the wounded child* by adding the concrete subject doctors worked. Option A infers that an explosion was working to save the wounded child. Option B never tells who was trying to save the wounded child.

3. Option A places the adverb *wildly* closest to the verb screamed, which it modifies. Both Options B and C incorrectly place the modifier away from the verb.

4. Option B corrects the modifier *looking through the file cabinets in the office* by placing it next to the detective who is doing the looking. Option A sounds as though the photographs were looking; Option C has no one doing the looking.

Appropriate Comparative and Superlative Degree Forms

When comparisons are made, the correct form of the adjective or adverb must be used. The comparative form is used for two items. The superlative form is used for more than two.

	Comparative	**Superlative**
slow	slower	slowest
young	younger	youngest
tall	taller	tallest

With some words, *more* and *most* are used to make comparisons instead of *er* and *est*.

quiet	more quiet	most quiet
energetic	more energetic	most energetic
quick	more quickly	most quickly

Comparisons must be made between similar structures or items. In the sentence, "My house is similar in color to Steve's," one house is being compared to another house as understood by the use of the possessive Steve's.

On the other hand, if the sentence reads "My house is similar in color to Steve," the comparison would be faulty because it would be comparing the house to Steve, not to Steve's house.

Error: Last year's rides at the carnival were bigger than this year.

Problem: In the sentence as it is worded above, the rides at the carnival are being compared to this year, not to this year's rides.

Correction: *Last year's rides at the carnival were bigger than this year's.*

PRACTICE EXERCISE – LOGICAL COMPARISONS

Choose the sentence that logically and correctly expresses the comparison.

1. A. This year's standards are higher than last year.
   B. This year's standards are more high than last year.
   C. This year's standards are higher than last year's.

2. A. Tom's attitudes are very different from his father's.
   B. Toms attitudes are very different from his father.
   C. Tom's attitudes are very different from his father.

3. A. John is the stronger member of the gymnastics team.
   B. John is the strongest member of the gymnastics team.
   C. John is the most strong member of the gymnastics team.

4. A. Tracy's book report was longer than Tony's.
   B. Tracy's book report was more long than Tony's.
   C. Tracy's book report was longer than Tony.

5. A. Becoming a lawyer is as difficult as, if not more difficult than, becoming a doctor.
   B. Becoming a lawyer is as difficult, if not more difficult than, becoming a doctor.
   C. Becoming a lawyer is difficult, if not more difficult than, becoming a doctor.

6. A. Better than any movie of the modern era, *Schindler's List* portrays the destructiveness of hate.
   B. More better than any movie of the modern era, *Schindler's List* portrays the destructiveness of hate.
   C. Better than any other movie of the modern era, *Schindler's List* portrays the destructiveness of hate.

Answer Key: Practice Exercise for Logical Comparisons

1. Option C is correct because the comparison is between this year's standards and last year's [standards is understood]. Option A compares the standards to last year. In Option B, the faulty comparative more high should be higher.

2. Option A is correct because Tom's attitudes are compared to his father's (*attitudes* is understood). Option B deletes the necessary apostrophe to show possession (Tom's), and the comparison is faulty with *attitudes* compared to father. While Option C uses the correct possessive, it retains the faulty comparison shown in Option B.

3. In Option B, John is correctly the strongest member of a team that consists of more than two people. Option A uses the comparative *stronger* (comparison of two items) rather than the superlative *strongest* (comparison of more than two). Option C uses a faulty superlative *most strong*.

4. Option A is correct because the comparison is between Tracy's book report and Tony's (book report). Option B uses the faulty comparative *more long* instead of *longer*. Option C wrongly compares Tracy's book report to Tony.

5. In Option A, the dual comparison is correctly stated: *as difficult as, if not more difficult than*. Remember to test the dual comparison by taking out the intervening comparison. Option B deletes the necessary *as* after the first difficult. Option C deletes the *as* before and after the first difficult.

6. Option C includes the necessary word *other* in the comparison better than any other movie. The comparison in Option A is not complete, and Option B uses a faulty comparative *more better*.

COMPETENCY 5.0 UNDERSTAND AND APPLY BASIC PRINCIPLES OF GOOD WRITING

Skill 5.1 Recognize the use of writing for different audiences and purposes (e.g., business letter, newspaper article, advertisement)

When authors set out to write a passage, they usually have a purpose for doing so. That purpose may be to simply give information that might be interesting or useful; it may be to persuade the reader to a point of view or to move the reader to act in a particular way; it may be to tell a story; or it may be to describe something in such a way that an experience becomes available to the reader through one of the five senses. Following are the primary devices for expressing a particular purpose in a piece of writing:

- **Basic expository writing** simply gives information not previously known about a topic or is used to explain or define one. Facts, examples, statistics, cause and effect, direct tone, objective rather than subjective delivery, and non-emotional information are presented in a formal manner.

- **Descriptive writing** centers on person, place, or object, using concrete and sensory words to create a mood or impression and arranging details in a chronological or spatial sequence.

- **Narrative writing** is developed using an incident or anecdote or related series of events. Chronology, the 5 W's, topic sentence, and conclusion are essential ingredients.

- **Persuasive writing** implies the writer's ability to select vocabulary and arrange facts and opinions in such a way as to direct the actions of the listener/reader. Persuasive writing may incorporate exposition and narration as they illustrate the main idea.

NCTE Beliefs about the Teaching of Writing

by the Writing Study Group of the NCTE Executive Committee
November 2004

1. ***Everyone has the capacity to write, writing can be taught, and teachers can help students become better writers.***
2. ***People learn to write by writing.***
3. ***Writing is a process.***
4. ***Writing is a tool for thinking.***
5. ***Writing grows out of many different purposes.***
6. ***Conventions of finished and edited texts are important to readers and therefore to writers.***
7. ***Writing and reading are related.***
8. ***Writing has a complex relationship to talk.***
9. ***Literate practices are embedded in complicated social relationships.***
10. ***Composing occurs in different modalities and technologies.***
11. ***Assessment of writing involves complex, informed, human judgment***

- **Journalistic writing** is theoretically free of author bias. When relaying information about an event, person, or thing, it should be factual and objective. Provide students with an opportunity to examine newspapers and create their own. Many newspapers have educational programs that are offered free to schools.

Two characteristics that determine language style are **degree of formality** and **word choice**. The most formal language does not use contractions or slang while the most informal language will probably feature a more casual use of common sayings and anecdotes. Formal language will use longer sentences and will not sound like a conversation. The most informal language will use shorter sentences (not necessarily simple sentences—but shorter constructions) and may sound like a conversation.

In both formal and informal writing, there exists a **tone**, the writer's attitude toward the material and/or readers. Tone may be playful, formal, intimate, angry, serious, ironic, outraged, baffled, tender, serene, depressed, and so on. The overall tone of a piece of writing is dictated by both the subject matter and the audience. Tone is related to the actual **word choice** which makes up the document, as we attach affective meanings to words, called their **connotations**. Gaining this conscious control over language makes it possible to use language appropriately in various situations and to evaluate its uses in literature and other forms of communication. By evoking the proper responses from readers or listeners, we can prompt them to take action.

Using the following questions is an excellent way to assess the audience and tone of a given piece of writing.

1. Who is your audience (friend, teacher, business person, someone else)?

2. How much does this person know about you and/or your topic?

3. What is your purpose (to prove an argument, to persuade, to amuse, to register a complaint, to ask for a raise, etc)?

4. What emotions do you have about the topic (nervous, happy, confident, angry, sad, no feelings at all)?
5. What emotions do you want to register with your audience (anger, nervousness, happiness, boredom, interest)?

6. What persona do you need to create in order to achieve your purpose?

7. What choice of language is best suited to achieving your purpose with your particular subject (slang, friendly but respectful, formal)?

8. What emotional quality do you want to transmit to achieve your purpose (matter of fact, informative, authoritative, inquisitive, sympathetic, angry), and to what degree do you want to express this tone?

Skill 5.2 Identify effective topic sentences and supporting details

Topic Sentences

Just as the essay must have an overall focus reflected in the thesis statement, each paragraph must have a central idea reflected in the topic sentence. A good topic sentence also provides transition from the previous paragraph and relates to the essay's thesis. Good topic sentences, therefore, provide unity throughout the essay.

Consider the following potential topic sentences. Be sure that each provides transition and clearly states the subject of the paragraph.

Topic Sentence 1: Computers are used in science.

Analysis: This sentence simply states the topic--computers used in science. It does not relate to the thesis or provide transition from the introduction. The reader still does not know how computers are used.

Topic Sentence 2: Now I will talk about computers used in science.

Analysis: Like the faulty "announcer" thesis statement, this "announcer" topic sentence is vague and merely names the topic.

Topic Sentence 3: First, computers used in science have improved our lives.

Analysis: The transition word *First* helps link the introduction and this paragraph. It adds unity to the essay. However, it does not give specifics about the improvement computers have made in our lives.

Topic Sentence 4: First used in scientific research and spaceflights, computers are now used extensively in the diagnosis and treatment of disease.

Analysis: This sentence is the most thorough and fluent. It provides specific areas that will be discussed in the paragraph and offers more than an announcement of the topic. The writer gives concrete information about the content of the paragraph that will follow.

Summary Guidelines for Writing Topic Sentences

1. **Specifically relate the topic to the thesis statement.**
2. **State clearly and concretely the subject of the paragraph**
3. **Provide some transition from the previous paragraph**
4. **Avoid topic sentences that are facts, questions, or announcers.**

Supporting Details

Because every good thesis has an assertion, you should offer specifics, facts, data, anecdotes, expert opinion, and other details to *show* or *prove* that assertion. While *you* know what you mean, your *reader* does not.

See also 2.2.

Skill 5.3 Recognize distracting details or material not relevant to the main idea of a paragraph or passage

The main idea of a passage may contain a wide variety of supporting information, but it is important that each sentence be related to the main idea. When a sentence contains information that bears little or no connection to the main idea, it is said to be **irrelevant**.

The following passage has several irrelevant sentences that are highlighted in bold

> The New City Planning Committee is proposing a new capitol building to represent the multicultural face of New City. **The current mayor is a Democrat.** The new capitol building will be on 10th street across from the grocery store and next to the Recreational Center. It will be within walking distance to the subway and bus depot, as the designers want to emphasize the importance of public transportation. Aesthetically, the building will have a contemporary design featuring a brushed-steel exterior and large, floor to ceiling windows. **It is important for employees to have a connection with the outside world even when they are in their offices.** Inside the building, the walls will be moveable. This will not only facilitate a multitude of creative floor plans, but it will also create a focus on open communication and flow of information. **It sounds a bit gimmicky to me.** Finally, the capitol will feature a large outdoor courtyard full of lush greenery and serene fountains. **Work will now seem like Club Med to those who work at the New City capitol!**

Skill 5.4 Recognize sentence fragments and run-on sentences

Fragments

Fragments occur (1) if word groups standing alone are missing either a subject or a verb, and (2) if word groups containing a subject and verb and standing alone are actually made dependent because of the use of subordinating conjunctions or relative pronouns.

Error: The teacher waiting for the class to complete the assignment.

Problem: This sentence is not complete because of the “ing” word alone does not function as a verb. When a helping verb is added (for example, was waiting), it will become a sentence.

Correction: *The teacher was waiting for the class to complete the assignment.*

Error: Until the last toy was removed from the floor.

Problem: Words such as “until,” ”because,” “although,” “when,” and “if” make a clause dependent and thus incapable of standing alone. An independent clause must be added to make the sentence complete.

Correction: *Until the last toy was removed from the floor, the kids could not go outside to play.*

Error: The city will close the public library. Because of a shortage of funds.

Problem: The problem is the same as above. The dependent clause must be joined to the independent clause.

Correction: *The city will close the public library because of a shortage of funds.*

Practice Exercise: Fragments

Choose the option that corrects the underlined portion(s) of the sentence. If no error exists, choose "No change is necessary."

1. Despite the lack of funds in the budget it was necessary to rebuild the roads that were damaged from the recent floods.

   A. budget: it
   B. budget, it
   C. budget; it
   D. No change is necessary

2. After determining that the fire was caused by faulty wiring, the building inspector said the construction company should be fined.

   A. wiring. The
   B. wiring the
   C. wiring; the
   D. No change is necessary

3. Many years after buying a grand piano Henry decided he'd rather play the violin instead.

   A. piano: Henry
   B. piano, Henry
   C. piano; Henry
   D. No change is necessary

4. Computers are being used more and more frequently. because of their capacity to store information.

   A. frequently because
   B. frequently, because
   C. frequently; because
   D. No change is necessary

5. Doug washed the floors every day. to keep them clean for the guests.

   A. every day to
   B. every day,
   C. every day;
   D. No change is necessary.

Answer Key: Practice Exercise for Fragments

1. Option B is correct. The clause that begins with *despite* is independent and must be separated with the clause that follows by a comma. Option A is incorrect because a colon is used to set off a list or to emphasize what follows. In Option C, a semicolon incorrectly suggests that the two clauses are dependent.

2. Option D is correct. A comma correctly separates the dependent clause *After...wiring* at the beginning of the sentence from the independent clause that follows. Option A incorrectly breaks the two clauses into separate sentences, while Options B omits the comma, and Option C incorrectly suggests that the phrase is an independent clause.

3. Option B is correct. The phrase *Henry decided...instead* must be joined to the independent clause. Option A incorrectly puts a colon before Henry decided, and Option C incorrectly separates the phrase as if it were an independent clause.

4. Option A is correct. The second clause *because...information* is dependent and must be joined to the first independent clause. Option B is incorrect because as the dependent clause comes at the end of the sentence, rather than at the beginning, a comma is not necessary. In Option C, a semi-colon incorrectly suggests that the two clauses are independent.

5. Option A is correct. The second clause *to keep...guests* is dependent and must be joined to the first independent clause. Option B is incorrect because as the dependent clause comes at the end of the sentence, rather than at the beginning, a comma is not necessary. In Option C, a semi-colon incorrectly suggests that the two clauses are independent.

Run-on Sentences and Comma Splices

Comma splices appear when two sentences are joined by only a comma. Fused sentences appear when two sentences are run together with no punctuation at all.

Error Dr. Sanders is a brilliant scientist, his research on genetic disorders won him a Nobel Prize.

Problem: A comma alone cannot join two independent clauses (complete sentences). The two clauses can be joined by a semi-colon, or they can be separated by a period.

Correction: *Dr. Sanders is a brilliant scientist; his research on genetic disorders won him a Nobel Prize.*

or

Dr. Sanders is a brilliant scientist. His research on genetic disorders won him a Nobel Prize.

Error: Florida is noted for its beaches they are long, sandy, and beautiful.

Problem: The first sentence ends with the word beaches, and the second sentence cannot be joined with the first. The fused sentence error can be corrected in several ways: (1) one clause may be made dependent on another with a subordinating conjunction or a relative pronoun; (2) a semi-colon may be used to combine two equally important ideas; (3) the two independent clauses may be separated by a period.

Correction: *Florida is noted for its beaches, which are long, sandy, and beautiful*

or

Florida is noted for its beaches; they are long, sandy, and beautiful.

or

Florida is noted for its beaches. They are long, sandy, and beautiful.

Error: The number of hotels has increased, however, the number of visitors has grown also.

Problem: The first sentence ends with the word increased, and a comma is not strong enough to connect it to the second sentence. The adverbial transition however does not function the same way as a coordinating conjunction and cannot be used with commas to link two sentences. Several different corrections are available.

Correction: *The number of hotels has increased; however, the number of visitors has grown also.*
[Two separate but closely related sentences are created with the use of the semicolon.]

or

The number of hotels has increased. However, the number of visitors has grown also.
[Two separate sentences are created.]

or

Although the number of hotels have increased, the number of visitors has grown also.
[One idea is made subordinate to the other and separated with a comma.]

or

T*he number of hotels have increased, but the number of visitors has grown, also.*
[The comma before the coordinating conjunction *but* is appropriate. The adverbial transition however does not function the same way as the coordinating conjunction but does.]

Practice Exercise: Fused Sentences and Comma Splices

Choose the option that corrects an error in the underlined portion(s). If no error exists, choose "No change is necessary."

1. Scientists are excited at the ability to clone a sheep; however, it is not yet known if the same can be done to humans.

    A. sheep, however,
    B. sheep. However,
    C. sheep, however;
    D. No change is necessary

2. Because of the rising cost of college tuition the federal government now offers special financial assistance, such as loans to students.

    A. tuition, the
    B. tuition; the
    C. such as loans
    D. No change is necessary.

3. As the number of homeless people continue to rise, the major cities like New York and Chicago, are now investing millions of dollars in low-income housing.

    A. rise. The major cities
    B. rise; the major cities
    C. New York and Chicago
    D. No change is necessary

4. Unlike in the 1950's, most households find the husband and wife *in many* different career fields working full-time to make ends meet.

    A. the 1950's; most
    B. the 1950's most
    C. ends meet, in many
    D. No change is necessary.

Answer Key: Practice Exercise for Comma Splices and Fused Sentences

1. Option B correctly separates two independent clauses. The comma in Option A after the word sheep creates a run-on sentence. The semi-colon in Option C does not separate the two clauses but occurs at an inappropriate point.

2. The comma in Option A correctly separates the independent clause and the dependent clause. The semi-colon in Option B is incorrect because one of the clauses is independent. Option C requires a comma to prevent a run-on sentence.

3. Option C is correct because a comma creates a run-on. Option A is incorrect because the first clause is dependent. The semi-colon in Option B incorrectly divides the dependent clause from the independent clause.

4. Option D correctly punctuates the sentence. Option A incorrectly uses a semi-colon. The lack of a comma in Option B violates the rule that an introductory phrase requires a comma after it. Option C puts a comma in an inappropriate place.

Skill 5.5 Demonstrate the ability to edit written text to improve grammar, sentence structure, and word usage

To help students improve their writing, you will want them to understand various techniques to revise text to achieve clarity and economy of expression.

Enhancing Interest

- Start out with an attention-grabbing introduction. This sets an engaging tone for the entire piece and will be more likely to pull readers in.
- Use dynamic vocabulary and varied sentence beginnings. Keep the readers on their toes. If they can predict what you are going to say next, switch it up.
- Avoid using clichés (as cold as ice, the best thing since sliced bread, nip it in the bud). These are easy shortcuts, but they are not interesting, memorable, or convincing.

Ensuring Understanding

- Avoid using the words "clearly," "obviously," and "undoubtedly." Often, what is clear or obvious to the author is not as apparent to the readers. Instead of using these words, make your point so strongly that it is clear on its own.
- Use the word that best fits the meaning you intend, even if it is longer or a little less common. Try to find a balance, and go with a familiar, yet precise, word.
- When in doubt, explain further.

Revising Sentences to Eliminate Wordiness, Ambiguity, and Redundancy

You may think this exercise is simply catching errors in spelling or word use, but you should reframe your thinking about revising and editing. This is an extremely important step that often is ignored. Some questions you should ask:

- Is the reasoning coherent?
- Is the point established?
- Does the introduction make the reader want to read this discourse?
- What is the thesis? Is it proven?
- What is the purpose? Is it clear? Is it useful, valuable, and interesting?
- Is the style of writing so wordy that it exhausts the reader and interferes with engagement?
- Is the writing so spare that it is boring?
- Are the sentences too uniform in structure?
- Are there too many simple sentences?
- Are too many of the complex sentences the same structure?

- Are the compounds truly compounds, or are they unbalanced?
- Are parallel structures truly parallel?
- If there are characters, are they believable?
- If there is dialogue, is it natural or stilted?
- Is the title appropriate?
- Does the writing show creativity, or is it boring?
- Is the language appropriate? Is it too formal? Too informal? If jargon is used, is it appropriate?

Studies have clearly demonstrated that the most fertile area in teaching writing is this one. If students can learn to revise their own work effectively, they are well on their way to becoming effective, mature writers. Word processing is an important tool for teaching this stage in the writing process. Microsoft Word has tracking features that make the revision exchanges between teachers and students more effective than ever before.

With strong research skills, students will find more information than they could possibly use so your task now is to help them eliminate irrelevant or unimportant information. The key is to focus on the thesis statement—what evidence will support the main point?

Techniques to Maintain Focus

- **Focus on a main point.** The point should be clear to readers, and all sentences in the paragraph should relate to it.

- **Start the paragraph with a topic sentence.** This should be a general, one-sentence summary of the paragraph's main point, relating back to the thesis and forward to the content of the paragraph. (A topic sentence is sometimes unnecessary if the paragraph continues a developing idea clearly introduced in a preceding paragraph, or if the paragraph appears in a narrative of events where generalizations might interrupt the flow of the story.)

- **Stick to the point.** Eliminate sentences that do not support the topic sentence.

- **Be flexible.** If you do not have enough evidence to support the claim of your topic sentence, do not fall into the trap of wandering or introducing new ideas within the paragraph. Either find more evidence, or adjust the topic sentence to corroborate with the evidence that is available.

> Learn more about
> **Editing and Proofreading Strategies for Revision**
> http://owl.english.purdue.edu/handouts/general/gl_edit.html

COMPETENCY 6.0 UNDERSTAND THE PROPER USE OF SPELLING, PUNCTUATION, AND CAPITALIZATION IN STANDARD AMERICAN ENGLISH

Skill 6.1 Identify and correcting errors in spelling

Spelling correctly is not always easy, because English not only uses an often inconsistent spelling system but also uses many words derived from other languages. Good spelling is important because incorrect spelling damages the physical appearance of writing and may puzzle your reader.

The following words are misspelled the most often.

1. commitment
2. succeed
3. necessary
4. connected
5. opportunity
6. embarrassed
7. occasionally
8. receive
9. their
10. accelerate
11. patience
12. obstinate
13. achievement
14. responsibility
15. prejudice
16. familiar
17. hindrance
18. controversial
19. publicity
20. prescription
21. possession
22. accumulate
23. hospitality
24. judgment
25. conscious
26. height
27. leisurely
28. shield
29. foreign
30. innovative
31. similar
32. proceed
33. contemporary
34. beneficial
35. attachment
36. guarantee
37. tropical
38. misfortune
39. particular
40. yield

Practice Exercise on ei/ie Words

Circle the correct spelling of the word in each parenthesis.

1. The (shield, shield) protected the gladiator from serious injury.
2. Tony (received, recieved) an award for his science project.
3. Our (neighbors, nieghbors), the Thomsons, are in the Witness Protection Program.
4. Janet's (friend, freind), Olivia, broke her leg while running the marathon.
5. She was unable to (conceive, concieve) a child after her miscarriage.
6. Rudolph the Red-Nosed (Riendeer, Reindeer) is my favorite Christmas song.
7. The farmer spent all day plowing his (feild, field).
8. Kat's (wieght, weight) loss plan failed, and she gained twenty pounds!
9. They couldn't (beleive, believe) how many people showed up for the concert.
10. Ruby's (niece, neice) was disappointed when the movie was sold out.

Answer Key: ei/ie Words

1. shield
2. received
3. neighbors
4. friend
5. conceive
6. reindeer
7. field
8. weight
9. believe
10. niece

Practice Exercise: Spelling Rules

Add suffixes to the following words and write the correct spelling form in the blanks.

1. swing + ing = ____________
2. use + able = ____________
3. choke + ing = ____________
4. furnish + ed = ____________
5. punish + ment = ____________
6. duty + ful = ____________
7. bereave + ment = ____________
8. shovel + ing = ____________
9. argue + ment = ____________
10. connect + ed = ____________
11. remember + ed = ____________
12. treat + able = ____________
13. marry + s = ____________
14. recycle + able = ____________
15. waste + ful = ____________
16. pray + ing = ____________
17. reconstruct + ing = ____________
18. outrage + ous = ____________

Answer Key: Spelling Rules Practice

1. swinging
2. useable
3. choking
4. furnished
5. punishment
6. dutiful
7. bereavement
8. shoveling
9. argument
10. connected
11. remembered
12. treatable
13. marries
14. recyclable
15. wasteful
16. praying
17. reconstructing
18. outrageous

Skill 6.2 Identifying and correcting errors in punctuation

Commas

Commas indicate a brief pause. They are used to set off dependent clauses and long introductory word groups, to separate words in a series, to set off incidental information that interrupts the flow of the sentence, and to separate independent clauses joined by conjunctions.

Error: After I finish my master's thesis I plan to work in Chicago.

Problem: A comma is needed after an introductory dependent clause containing a subject and verb.

Correction: *After I finish my master's thesis, I plan to work in Chicago.*

Error: I washed waxed and vacuumed my car today.

Problem: Nouns, phrases, or clauses in a list, as well as two or more coordinate adjectives that modify one word should be separated by commas. Although the word and is sometimes considered optional, it is often necessary to clarify the meaning.

Correction: *I washed, waxed, and vacuumed my car today.*

Error: She was a talented dancer but she is mostly remembered for her singing ability.

Problem: A comma is needed before a conjunction that joins two independent clauses (complete sentences).

Correction: *She was a talented dancer, but she is mostly remembered for her singing ability.*

Error: This incident is I think typical of what can happen when the community remains so divided.

Problem: Commas are needed between nonessential words or words that interrupt the main clause.

Correction: *This incident is, I think, typical of what can happen when the community remains so divided.*

Semicolons and Colons

Semicolons are needed to separate two or more closely related independent clauses when the second clause is introduced by a transitional adverb. (These clauses may also be written as separate sentences, preferably by placing the adverb within the second sentence). **Colons** are used to introduce lists and to emphasize what follows.

Error: I climbed to the top of the mountain, it took me three hours.

Problem: A comma alone cannot separate two independent clauses. Instead a semicolon is needed to separate two related sentences.

Correction: *I climbed to the top of the mountain; it took me three hours.*

Error: In the movie, asteroids destroyed Dallas, Texas, Kansas City, Missouri, and Boston, Massachusetts.

Problem: Semicolons are needed to separate items in a series that already contains internal punctuation.

Correction: *In the movie, asteroids destroyed Dallas, Texas; Kansas City, Missouri; and Boston, Massachusetts.*

Error: Essays will receive the following grades, A for excellent, B for good, C for average, and D for unsatisfactory.

Problem: A colon is needed to emphasize the information or list that follows.

Correction: *Essays will receive the following grades: A for excellent, B for good, C for average, and D for unsatisfactory.*

Error: The school carnival included: amusement rides, clowns, food booths, and a variety of games.

Problem: The material preceding the colon and the list that follows is not a complete sentence. Do not separate a verb (or preposition) from the object.

Correction: *The school carnival included amusement rides ,clowns, food booths, and a variety of games.*

Apostrophes

Apostrophes are used to show either contractions or possession.

Error: She shouldnt be permitted to smoke cigarettes in the building.

Problem: An apostrophe is needed in a contraction in place of the missing letter.

Correction: *She shouldn't be permitted to smoke cigarettes in the building.*

Error: My cousins motorcycle was stolen from his driveway.

Problem: An apostrophe is needed to show possession.

Correction: *My cousin's motorcycle was stolen from his driveway.*
(Note: The use of the apostrophe before the letter "*s*" means that there is just one cousin. The plural form would read the following way: My cousins' motorcycle was stolen from their driveway.)

Error: The childrens new kindergarten teacher was also a singer.

Problem: An apostrophe is needed to show possession.

Correction: *The children's new kindergarten teacher was also a singer.* (Note: children is plural, so the apostrophe comes between the *n* and the s.)

Error: Children screams could be heard for miles.

Problem: An apostrophe and the letter *s* are needed in the sentence to show whose screams it is.

Correction: *Children's screams could he heard for miles.* (Note: children is plural, so the apostrophe comes between the *n* and the *s.)*

Quotation Marks

The more troublesome punctuation marks involve the use of quotations.

Using Terminal Punctuation in Relation to Quotation Marks: In a quoted statement that is either declarative or imperative, place the period inside the closing quotation marks.

"The airplane crashed on the runway during takeoff."

If the quotation is followed by other words in the sentence, place a comma inside the closing quotations marks and a period at the end of the sentence.

"The airplane crashed on the runway during takeoff," said the announcer.

In most instances in which a quoted title or expression occurs at the end of a sentence, the period is placed before either the single or double quotation marks.

"The middle school readers were unprepared to understand Bryant's poem 'Thanatopsis.'"

Early book-length adventure stories like *Don Quixote* and *The Three Musketeers* were known as "picaresque novels."

There is an instance in which the final quotation mark would precede the period - if the content of the sentence were about a speech or quote so that the understanding of the meaning would be confused by the placement of the period.

The first thing out of his mouth was "Hi, I'm home." *but*
The first line of his speech began "I arrived home to an empty house".

In sentences that are interrogatory or exclamatory, the question mark or exclamation point should be positioned outside the closing quotation marks if the quote itself is a statement or command or cited title.

Who decided to lead us in the recitation of the "Pledge of Allegiance"?

Why was Tillie shaking as she began her recitation, "Once upon a midnight dreary..."?

I was embarrassed when Mrs. White said, "Your slip is showing"!

In sentences that are declarative but the quotation is a question or an exclamation, place the question mark or exclamation point inside the quotation marks.

The hall monitor yelled, "Fire! Fire!"

"Fire! Fire!" yelled the hall monitor.

Cory shrieked, "Is there a mouse in the room?" (In this instance, the question supersedes the exclamation.)

Using Double Quotation Marks with Other Punctuation

Quotations - whether words, phrases, or clauses - should be punctuated according to the rules of the grammatical function they serve in the sentence.

The works of Shakespeare, "the bard of Avon," have been contested as originating with other authors.

"You'll get my money," the old man warned, "when 'Hell freezes over'."

Sheila cited the passage that began "Four score and seven years ago...." (Note the ellipsis followed by an enclosed period.)

Old Ironsides inspired the preservation of the U.S.S. Constitution.

Use quotation marks to enclose the titles of shorter works: songs, short poems, short stories, essays, and chapters of books. (See "Using Italics" for punctuating longer titles.)

> "The Tell-Tale Heart" - short story
> "Casey at the Bat" - poem
> "America the Beautiful" - song

Using Dashes and Italics

Place dashes to denote sudden breaks in thought.

> Some periods in literature - the Romantic Age, for example - spanned different time periods in different countries.

Use dashes instead of commas if commas are already used elsewhere in the sentence for amplification or explanation.

> The Fireside Poets included three Brahmans - James Russell Lowell, Henry David Wadsworth, Oliver Wendell Holmes - and John Greenleaf Whittier.

Use italics to punctuate the titles of long works of literature, names of periodical publications, musical scores, works of art and motion picture television, and radio programs. (When unable to write in italics, you can instruct students to underline in their own writing where italics would be appropriate.)

The Idylls of the King	*Hiawatha*	*The Sound and the Fury*
Mary Poppins	*Newsweek*	*The Nutcracker Suite*

Skill 6.3 Identify and correcting errors in capitalization

Capitalization

Check out this
Guide to Grammar and Writing
http://grammar.ccc.commnet.edu/grammar/

Capitalize all proper names of persons (including specific organizations or agencies of government); places (countries, states, cities, parks, and specific geographical areas); and things (political parties, structures, historical and cultural terms, and calendar and time designations); and religious terms (any deity, revered person or group, sacred writings).

Percy Bysshe Shelley, Argentina, Mount Rainier National Park, Grand Canyon, League of Nations, the Sears Tower, Birmingham, Lyric Theater, Americans, Midwesterners, Democrats, Renaissance, Boy Scouts of America, Easter, God, Bible, Dead Sea Scrolls, Koran

Capitalize proper adjectives and titles used with proper names.

California gold rush, President John Adams, French fries, Homeric epic, Romanesque architecture, Senator John Glenn

Note: Some words that represent titles and offices are not capitalized unless used with a proper name.

Capitalized	Not Capitalized
Congressman McKay	the congressman from Florida
Commander Alger	commander of the Pacific Fleet
Queen Elizabeth	the queen of England

Capitalize all main words in titles of works of literature, art, and music.

Error: Emma went to Dr. Peters for treatment since her own Doctor was on vacation.

Problem: The use of capital letters with Emma and Dr .Peters is correct since they are specific (proper) names; the title Dr. is also capitalized. However, the word doctor is not a specific name and should not be capitalized.

Correction: *Emma went to Dr. Peters for treatment since her own doctor was on vacation.*

Error: Our Winter Break does not start until next wednesday.

Problem: Days of the week are capitalized, but seasons are not capitalized.

Correction: *Our winter break does not start until next Wednesday.*

Error: The exchange student from israel who came to study biochemistry spoke spanish very well.

Problem: Languages and the names of countries are always capitalized. Courses are also capitalized when they refer to a specific course; they are not capitalized when they refer to courses in general.

Correction: *The exchange student from Israel who came to study Biochemistry spoke Spanish very well.*

Practice Exercise: Capitalization and Punctuation

Choose the option that corrects an error in the underlined portion(s). If no error exists, choose "No change is necessary."

1. Greenpeace is an Organization that works to preserve the world's environment.

   A. greenpeace
   B. organization
   C. worlds
   D. No change is necessary.

2. When our class travels to France next year, we will see the country's many famous landmarks.

   A. france
   B. year; we
   C. countries
   D. No change is necessary.

3. New York City, the heaviest populated city in America has more than eight million people living there everyday.

   A. new york city
   B. in America, has
   C. Everyday
   D. No change is necessary.

4. The television show The X-Files has gained a huge following because it focuses on paranormal phenomena, extraterrestrial life, and the oddities of human existence.

   A. Television
   B. following, because
   C. Human existence
   D. No change is necessary.

5. Being a Policeman requires having many qualities: physical agility, good reflexes, and the ability to make quick decisions.

   A. policeman
   B. qualities;
   C. agility:
   D. No change is necessary

Answer Key: Practice Exercise for Capitalization and Punctuation

1. Option B is correct. In the sentence, the word organization does not need to be capitalized because it is a general noun. In Option A, the name of the organization should be capitalized. In Option C, the apostrophe is used to show that one world is being protected, not more than one.

2. Option D is correct. In Option A, France is capitalized because it is the name of a country. In Option B, the comma, not the semi-colon, should separate a dependent clause from the main clause. In Option C, the use of an apostrophe and an *s* indicates only one country is being visited.

3. Option B is correct. In Option A, New York City is capitalized because it is the name of a place. In Option B, a comma is needed to separate the noun America, from the verb has. In Option C, the noun everyday needs no capitalization.

4. Option D is correct. In Option A, television does not need to be capitalized because it is a noun. In Option B, a comma is necessary to separate an independent clause from the main clause. In Option C, human existence is a general term that does not need capitalization.

5. Option A is correct. In Option A, policeman does not need to be capitalized because it is a general noun. In Option B, a colon, not a semi-colon, is needed because the rest of the sentence is related to the main clause. In Option C, a comma, not a colon, is needed to separate the adjectives.

SAMPLE TEST: WRITING

DIRECTIONS : *The passage below contains many errors. Read the passage. Then answer each test item by choosing the option that corrects an error in the underlined portion(s). No more than one underlined error will appear in each item. If no error exists, choose "No change is necessary."*

Climbing to the top of Mount Everest is an adventure. One which everyone--whether physically fit or not--seems eager to try. The trail stretches for miles; the cold temperatures are usually frigid and brutal.

Climbers must endure severel barriers on the way, including other hikers, steep jagged rocks, and lots of snow. Plus, climbers often find the most grueling part of the trip is their climb back down, just when they are feeling greatly exhausted. Climbers who take precautions are likely to find the ascent less arduous than the unprepared. By donning heavy flannel shirts, gloves, and hats, climbers prevented hypothermia, as well as simple frostbite. A pair of rugged boots is also one of the necesities. If climbers are to avoid becoming dehydrated, there is beverages available for them to transport as well.

Once climbers are completely ready to begin their lengthy journey, they can comfortable enjoy the wonderful scenery. Wide rock formations dazzle the observers eyes with shades of gray and white, while the peak forms a triangle that seems to touch the sky. Each of the climbers are reminded of the splendor and magnifisence of Gods great Earth.

1. **Plus, climbers often find the most grueling part of the trip is <u>their</u> climb back <u>down, just</u> when they <u>are</u> feeling greatly exhausted. (Skill 4.3, Average Rigor)**

   A. his
   B. down; just
   C. were
   D. No change is necessary.

2. **By donning heavy flannel shirts, boots, and <u>hats,</u> <u>climbers</u> <u>prevented</u> hypothermia, as well as simple frostbite. (Skill 4.3, Rigorous)**

   A. hats climbers
   B. can prevent
   C. hypothermia;
   D. No change is necessary.

3. **If climbers are to avoid becoming dehydrated, there is beverages available for them to transport as well. (Skill 4.3, Average Rigor)**

A. becomming
B. are
C. him
D. No change is necessary.

4. **Each of the climbers are reminded of the splendor and magnifisence of God's great Earth. (Skill 4.3, Rigorous)**

A. is
B. magnifisence
C. Gods
D. No change is necessary.

5. **Climbers who take precautions are likely to find the ascent less difficult than the unprepared. (Skill 4.5, Rigorous)**

A. Climbers, who
B. least difficult
C. then
D. No change is necessary.

6. **Once climbers are completely prepared for their lengthy journey, they can comfortable enjoy the wonderful scenery. (Skill 4.5, Rigorous)**

A. they're
B. journey; they
C. comfortably
D. No change is necessary.

7. **A pair of rugged boots is also one of the necesities. (Skill 6.1, Easy)**

A. are
B. also, one
C. necessities
D. No change is necessary.

8. **Climbers must endure severel barriers on the way, including other hikers, steep jagged rocks, and lots of snow. (Skill 6.1, Easy)**

A. several
B. on the way: including
C. hikers'
D. No change is necessary,

9. **Wide rock formations dazzle the observers eyes with shades of gray and white, while the peak forms a triangle that seems to touch the sky. (Skill 6.2, Rigorous)**

A. observers' eyes
B. white; while
C. formed
D. No change is necessary.

10. **Climbing to the top of Mount Everest is an adventure. One which everyone —whether physically fit or not—seems eager to try. (Skill 6.2, Average Rigor)**

A. adventure, one
B. people, whether
C. seem
D. No change is necessary,

11. **The trail stretches for miles, the cold temperatures are usually frigid and brutal. (Skill 6.2, Rigorous)**

A. trails
B. miles;
C. usual
D. No change is necessary,

DIRECTIONS: ***The passage below contains several errors. Read the passage. Then answer each test item by choosing the option that corrects an error in the underlined portion(s). No more than one underlined error will appear in each item. If no error exists, choose "No change is necessary."***

Every job places different kinds of demands on their employees. For example, whereas such jobs as accounting and bookkeeping require mathematical ability; graphic design requires creative/artistic ability.

Doing good at one job does not usually guarantee success at another. However, one of the elements crucial to all jobs are especially notable: the chance to accomplish a goal.

The accomplishment of the employees varies according to the job. In many jobs the employees become accustom to the accomplishment provided by the work they do every day.

In medicine, for example, every doctor tests him self by treating badly injured or critically ill people. In the operating room, a team of Surgeons, is responsible for operating on many of these patients. In addition to the feeling of accomplishment that the workers achieve, some jobs also give a sense of identity to the employees'. Profesions like law, education, and sales offer huge financial and emotional rewards. Politicians are public servants: who work for the federal and state governments. President bush is basically employed by the American people to make laws and run the country.

Finally; the contributions that employees make to their companies and to the world cannot be taken for granted. Through their work, employees are performing a service for their employers and are contributing something to the world.

12. **For example, whereas such jobs as accounting and bookkeeping require mathematical ability; graphic design requires creative/artistic ability. (Skill 4.1, 4.3 and 4.5, Average Rigor)**

A. For example
B. whereas,
C. ability,
D. No change is necessary.

13. **Every job places different kinds of demands on their employees. (Skill 4.3 and 4.4, Average Rigor)**

A. place
B. its
C. employes
D. No change is necessary.

14. **Doing good at one job does not usually guarantee success at another. (Skill 4.3 and 4.5, Average Rigor)**

A. well
B. usualy
C. succeeding
D. No change is necessary.

15. **However, one of the elements crucial to all jobs are especially notable: the accomplishment of a goal. (Skill 4.3 and 6.2, Average Rigor)**

A. However
B. is
C. notable;
D. No change is necessary.

16. **The accomplishment of the employees varies according to the job. (Skill 4.3, Average Rigor)**

A. accomplishment,
B. employee's
C. vary
D. No change is necessary.

17. **In many jobs the employees become accustom to the accomplishment provided by the work they do every day. (Skill 4.3, Average Rigor)**

A. became
B. accustomed
C. provides
D. No change is necessary.

18. **In medicine, for example, every doctor tests him self by treating badly injured and critically ill people. (Skill 4.3 and 4.4, Rigorous)**

A. test
B. himself
C. critical
D. No change is necessary.

19. **In addition to the feeling of accomplishment that the workers achieve, some jobs also give a sense of self-identity to the employees'. (Skill 4.3, 6.1 and 6.2, Average Rigor)**

A. acheive
B. gave
C. employees
D. No change is necessary.

20. **Profesions like law, education, and sales offer huge financial and emotional rewards. (Skill 4.3, 6.1, and 6.2, Rigorous)**

A. Professions
B. education;
C. offered
D. No change is necessary.

21. **Politicians are public servants: who work for the federal and state governments. (Skill 4.3, Easy)**

A. were
B. servants who
C. worked
D. No change is necessary.

22. **Finally; the contributions that employees make to their companies and to the world cannot be taken for granted. (Skill 4.3, 6.1, and 6.2, Rigorous)**

A. Finally,
B. their
C. took
D. No change is necessary.

23. **In the operating room, a team of Surgeons, is responsible for operating on many of these patients. (Skill 4.4, 6.2 and 6.3, Rigorous)**

A. operating room:
B. surgeons is
C. those
D. No change is necessary.

24. **President bush is basically employed by the American people to make laws and run the country. (Skill 6.3, Easy)**

A. Bush
B. to
C. made
D. No change is necessary .

DIRECTIONS: ***For the underlined sentence(s), choose the option that expresses the meaning with the most fluency and the clearest logic within the context. If the underlined sentence should not be changed, choose Option A, which shows no change.***

25. **Selecting members of a President's cabinet can often be an aggravating process. Either there are too many or too few qualified candidates for a certain position, and then they have to be confirmed by the Senate, where there is the possibility of rejection. (Skill 5.1, Easy)**

A. Either there are too many or too few qualified candidate for a certain position, and then they have to be confirmed by the Senate, where there is the possibility of rejection.

B. Qualified candidates for certain positions face the possibility of rejection, when they have to be confirmed by the Senate.

C. The Senate has to confirm qualified candidates, who face the possibility of rejection.

D. Because the Senate has to confirm qualified candidates; they face the possibility of rejection.

ANSWER KEY: WRITING

1. D
2. B
3. B
4. A
5. D
6. C
7. C
8. A
9. A
10. A
11. B
12. C
13. B
14. A
15. B
16. C
17. B
18. B
19. C
20. A
21. B
22. A
23. B
24. A
25. C

RIGOR TABLE: WRITING

Easy	Average Rigor	Rigorous
Question #s – 7, 8, 21, 24, 25	Question #s – 1, 3, 10, 12, 13, 14, 15, 16, 17, 19	Question #s-2, 4, 5, 6, 9, 11, 18, 20, 22, 23

RATIONALES FOR SAMPLE QUESTIONS: WRITING

DIRECTIONS : ***The passage below contains many errors. Read the passage. Then answer each test item by choosing the option that corrects an error in the underlined portion(s). No more than one underlined error will appear in each item. If no error exists, choose "No change is necessary."***

Climbing to the top of Mount Everest is an adventure. One which everyone--whether physically fit or not--seems eager to try. The trail stretches for miles, the cold temperatures are usually frigid and brutal.

Climbers must endure severel barriers on the way, including other hikers, steep jagged rocks, and lots of snow. Plus, climbers often find the most grueling part of the trip is their climb back down, just when they are feeling greatly exhausted. Climbers who take precautions are likely to find the ascent less arduous than the unprepared. By donning heavy flannel shirts, gloves, and hats, climbers prevented hypothermia, as well as simple frostbite. A pair of rugged boots is also one of the necesities. If climbers are to avoid becoming dehydrated, there is beverages available for them to transport as well.

Once climbers are completely ready to begin their lengthy journey, they can comfortable enjoy the wonderful scenery. Wide rock formations dazzle the observers eyes with shades of gray and white, while the peak forms a triangle that seems to touch the sky. Each of the climbers are reminded of the splendor and magnifisence of Gods great Earth.

1. **Plus, climbers often find the most grueling part of the trip is their climb back down, just when they are feeling greatly exhausted. (Skill 4.3, Average Rigor)**

   A. his
   B. down; just
   C. were
   D. No change is necessary.

The answer is D. The present tense must be used consistently throughout, therefore Option C is incorrect. Option A is incorrect because the singular pronoun *his* does not agree with the plural antecedent *climbers*. Option B is incorrect because a comma, not a semicolon, is needed to separate the dependent clause from the main clause.

2. **By donning heavy flannel shirts, boots, and hats, climbers prevented hypothermia, as well as simple frostbite. (Skill 4.3, Rigorous)**

A. hats climbers
B. can prevent
C. hypothermia;
D. No change is necessary.

The answer is B. The verb *prevented* is in the past tense and must be changed to the present *can prevent* to be consistent. Option A is incorrect because a comma is needed after a long introductory phrase. Option C is incorrect because the semicolon creates a fragment of the phrase *as well as simple frostbite*.

3. **If climbers are to avoid becoming dehydrated, there is beverages available for them to transport as well. (Skill 4.3, Average Rigor)**

A. becomming
B. are
C. him
D. No change is necessary.

The answer is B. The plural verb *are* must be used with the plural subject *beverages*. Option A is incorrect because *becoming* has only one m. Option C is incorrect because the plural pronoun *them* is needed to agree with the referent *climbers*.

4. **Each of the climbers are reminded of the splendor and magnifisence of God's great Earth. (Skill 4.3, Rigorous)**

A. is
B. magnifisence
C. Gods
D. No change is necessary.

The answer is A. The singular verb *is* agrees with the singular subject *each*. Option B is incorrect because *magnificence* is misspelled. Option C is incorrect because an apostrophe is needed to show possession.

5. **Climbers who take precautions are likely to find the ascent less difficult than the unprepared. (Skill 4.5, Rigorous)**

A. Climbers, who
B. least difficult
C. then
D. No change is necessary.

The answer is D. No change is needed. Option A is incorrect because a comma would make the phrase *who take precautions* seem less restrictive or less essential to the sentence. Option B is incorrect because *less* is appropriate when two items--the prepared and the unprepared--are compared. Option C is incorrect because the comparative adverb *than*, not *then*, is needed.

6. **Once climbers are completely prepared for their lengthy journey, they can comfortable enjoy the wonderful scenery. (Skill 4.5, Rigorous)**

A. they're
B. journey; they
C. comfortably
D. No change is necessary.

The answer is C. The adverb form *comfortably* is needed to modify the verb phrase *can enjoy*. Option A is incorrect because the possessive plural pronoun is spelled *their*. Option B is incorrect because a semi-colon would make the first half of the item seem like an independent clause when the subordinating conjunction *once* makes that clause dependent.

7. **A pair of rugged boots is also one of the necesities. (Skill 6.1, Easy)**

A. are
B. also, one
C. necessities
D. No change is necessary.

The answer is C. The word *necessities* is misspelled in the text. Option A is incorrect because the singular verb is must agree with the singular noun *pair* (a collective singular). Option B is incorrect because *if also* is set off with commas (potential correction), it should be set off on both sides.

8. Climbers must endure severel barriers on the way, including other hikers, steep jagged rocks, and lots of snow. (Skill 6.1, Easy)

A. several
B. on the way: including
C. hikers'
D. No change is necessary,

The answer is A. The word *several* is misspelled in the text. Option B is incorrect because a comma, not a colon, is needed to set off the modifying phrase. Option C is incorrect because no apostrophe is needed after *hikers* since possession is not involved.

9. Wide rock formations dazzle the observers eyes with shades of gray and white, while the peak forms a triangle that seems to touch the sky. (Skill 6.2, Rigorous)

A. observers' eyes
B. white; while
C. formed
D. No change is necessary.

The answer is A. An apostrophe is needed to show the plural possessive form *observers' eyes*. Option B is incorrect because the semicolon would make the second half of the item seem like an independent clause when the subordinating conjunction *while* makes that clause dependent. Option C is incorrect because *formed* is in the wrong tense.

10. Climbing to the top of Mount Everest is an adventure. One which everyone —whether physically fit or not—seems eager to try. (Skill 6.2, Average Rigor)

A. adventure, one
B. people, whether
C. seem
D. No change is necessary,

The answer is A. A comma is needed between *adventure* and *one* to avoid creating a fragment of the second part. In Option B, a comma after *everyone* would not be appropriate when the dash is used on the other side of *not*. In Option C, the singular verb *seems* is needed to agree with the singular subject *everyone*.

11. The trail stretches for miles, the cold temperatures are usually frigid and brutal. (Skill 6.2, Rigorous)

A. trails
B. miles;
C. usual
D. No change is necessary,

The answer is B. A semicolon, not a comma, is needed to separate the first independent clause from the second independent clause. Option A is incorrect because the plural subject *trails* needs the singular verb *stretch.* Option C is incorrect because the adverb form *usually* is needed to modify the adjective *frigid.*

DIRECTIONS: ***The passage below contains several errors. Read the passage. Then answer each test item by choosing the option that corrects an error in the underlined portion(s). No more than one underlined error will appear in each item. If no error exists, choose "No change is necessary."***

Every job places different kinds of demands on their employees. For example, whereas such jobs as accounting and bookkeeping require mathematical ability; graphic design requires creative/artistic ability.

Doing good at one job does not usually guarantee success at another. However, one of the elements crucial to all jobs are especially notable: the chance to accomplish a goal.

The accomplishment of the employees varies according to the job. In many jobs the employees become accustom to the accomplishment provided by the work they do every day.

In medicine, for example, every doctor tests him self by treating badly injured or critically ill people. In the operating room, a team of Surgeons, is responsible for operating on many of these patients. In addition to the feeling of accomplishment that the workers achieve, some jobs also give a sense of identity to the employees'. Profesions like law, education, and sales offer huge financial and emotional rewards. Politicians are public servants: who work for the federal and state governments. President bush is basically employed by the American people to make laws and run the country.

Finally; the contributions that employees make to their companies and to the world cannot be taken for granted. Through their work, employees are performing a service for their employers and are contributing something to the world.

12. For example, whereas such jobs as accounting and bookkeeping require mathematical ability; graphic design requires creative/artistic ability. (Skill 4.1, 4.3 and 4.5, Average Rigor)

A. For example
B. whereas,
C. ability,
D. No change is necessary.

The answer is C. An introductory dependent clause is set off with a comma, not a semicolon. Option A is incorrect because the transitional phrase *for example* should be set off with a comma. Option B is incorrect because the adverb *whereas* functions like *while* and does not take a comma after it.

13. Every job places different kinds of demands on their employees. (Skill 4.3 and 4.4, Average Rigor)

A. place
B. its
C. employes
D. No change is necessary.

The answer is B. The singular possessive pronoun *its* must agree with its antecedent *job*, which is singular also. Option A is incorrect because *place* is a plural form and the subject, *job*, is singular. Option C is incorrect because the correct spelling of employees is given in the sentence.

14. Doing good at one job does not usually guarantee success at another. (Skill 4.3 and 4.5, Average Rigor)

A. well
B. usualy
C. succeeding
D. No change is necessary.

The answer is A. The adverb *well* modifies the word *doing*. Option B is incorrect because *usually* is spelled correctly in the sentence. Option C is incorrect because *succeeding* is in the wrong tense.

15. However, one of the elements crucial to all jobs are especially notable: the accomplishment of a goal. (Skill 4.3 and 6.2, Average Rigor)

A. However
B. is
C. notable;
D. No change is necessary.

The answer is B. The singular verb *is* is needed to agree with the singular subject *one.* Option A is incorrect because a comma is needed to set off the transitional word *however.* Option C is incorrect because a colon, not a semicolon, is needed to set off an item.

16. The accomplishment of the employees varies according to the job. (Skill 4.3, Average Rigor)

A. accomplishment,
B. employee's
C. vary
D. No change is necessary.

The answer is C. The singular verb *vary* is needed to agree with the singular subject *accomplishment.* Option A is incorrect because a comma after *accomplishment* would suggest that the modifying phrase of the employees is additional instead of essential. Option B is incorrect because employees is not possessive.

17. In many jobs the employees become accustom to the accomplishment provided by the work they do every day. (Skill 4.3, Average Rigor)

A. became
B. accustomed
C. provides
D. No change is necessary.

The answer is B. The past participle *accustomed* is needed with the verb *become.* Option A is incorrect because the verb tense does not need to change to the past *became.* Option C is incorrect because *provides* is the wrong tense.

18. In medicine, for example, every doctor tests him self by treating badly injured and critically ill people. (Skill 4.3 and 4.4, Rigorous)

A. test
B. himself
C. critical
D. No change is necessary.

The answer is B. The reflexive pronoun *himself* is needed. (Him self is nonstandard and never correct.) Option A is incorrect because the singular verb test is needed to agree with the singular subject doctor. Option C is incorrect because the adverb *critically* is needed to modify the verb *ill.*

19. In addition to the feeling of accomplishment that the workers achieve, some jobs also give a sense of self-identity to the employees'. (Skill 4.3, 6.1 and 6.2, Average Rigor)

A. acheive
B. gave
C. employees
D. No change is necessary.

The answer is C. Option C is correct because *employees* is not possessive. Option A is incorrect because *achieve* is spelled correctly in the sentence. Option B is incorrect because *gave* is the wrong tense.

20. Profesions like law, education, and sales offer huge financial and emotional rewards. (Skill 4.3, 6.1, and 6.2, Rigorous)

A. Professions
B. education;
C. offered
D. No change is necessary.

The answer is A. Option A is correct because *professions* is misspelled in the sentence. Option B is incorrect because a comma, not a semi-colon, is needed after *education*. In Option C, *offered*, is in the wrong tense.

21. Politicians are public servants: who work for the federal and state governments. (Skill 4.3, Easy)

A. were
B. servants who
C. worked
D. No change is necessary.

The answer is B. A colon is not needed to set off the introduction of the sentence. In Option A, *were*, is the incorrect tense of the verb. In Option C, *worked*, is in the wrong tense.

22. Finally; the contributions that employees make to their companies and to the world cannot be taken for granted. (Skill 4.3, 6.1, and 6.2, Rigorous)

A. Finally,
B. their
C. took
D. No change is necessary.

The answer is A. A comma is needed to separate *Finally* from the rest of the sentence. Finally is a preposition which usually heads a dependent sentence, hence a comma is needed. Option B is incorrect because *their* is misspelled. Option C is incorrect because *took* is the wrong form of the verb.

23. In the operating room, a team of Surgeons, is responsible for operating on many of these patients. (Skill 4.4, 6.2 and 6.3, Rigorous)

A. operating room:
B. surgeons is
C. those
D. No change is necessary.

The answer is B. *Surgeons* is not a proper name so it does not need to be capitalized. A comma is not needed to break up a team of surgeons from the rest of the sentence. Option A is incorrect because a comma, not a colon, is needed to set off an item. Option C is incorrect because *those* is an incorrect pronoun.

24. President bush is basically employed by the American people to make laws and run the country. (Skill 6.3, Easy)

A. Bush
B. to
C. made
D. No change is necessary .

The answer is A. *Bush* is a proper name and should be capitalized. Option B, *to*, does not fit with the verb *employed.* Option C uses the wrong form of the verb, *make.*

DIRECTIONS: ***For the underlined sentence(s), choose the option that expresses the meaning with the most fluency and the clearest logic within the context. If the underlined sentence should not be changed, choose Option A, which shows no change.***

25. Selecting members of a President's cabinet can often be an aggravating process. Either there are too many or too few qualified candidates for a certain position, and then they have to be confirmed by the Senate, where there is the possibility of rejection. (Skill 5.1, Easy)

A. Either there are too many or too few qualified candidate for a certain position, and then they have to be confirmed by the Senate, where there is the possibility of rejection.

B. Qualified candidates for certain positions face the possibility of rejection, when they have to be confirmed by the Senate.

C. The Senate has to confirm qualified candidates, who face the possibility of rejection.

D. Because the Senate has to confirm qualified candidates; they face the possibility of rejection.

The answer is C. Option C is the most straightforward and concise sentence. Option A is too unwieldy with the wordy *Either...or* phrase at the beginning. Option B doesn't make clear the fact that candidates face rejection by the Senate. Option D illogically implies that candidates face rejection because they have to be confirmed by the Senate.

SUBAREA III. **MATHEMATICS**

COMPETENCY 7.0 UNDERSTAND NUMBER SENSE AND BASIC ALGEBRA

Skill 7.1 Demonstrate the ability to perform basic addition, subtraction, multiplication, and division of whole numbers, fractions, and decimals

Whole numbers are natural numbers and zero.
0, 1, 2, 3, ,4 ,5 ,6 ...

A **fraction** is an expression of numbers in the form of x/y, where ***x*** is the numerator and ***y*** is the denominator, which cannot be zero.

Example: $\frac{3}{7}$ 3 is the **numerator**; 7 is the **denominator**

If the fraction has common factors for the numerator and denominator, divide both by the common factor to reduce the fraction to its lowest form.

Example:

$$\frac{13}{39}=\frac{1\times 13}{3\times 13}=\frac{1}{3}$$ Divide by the common factor 13

Decimals = deci = part of ten. To find the decimal equivalent of a fraction, use the denominator to divide the numerator, as shown in the following example.

Example: Find the decimal equivalent of $\frac{7}{10}$.
Since 10 cannot divide into 7 evenly,

$$\frac{7}{10}=0.7$$

Rational numbers can be expressed as the ratio of two integers, $\frac{a}{b}$ where b $\neq$ 0. For example $\frac{2}{3}$, $-\frac{4}{5}$, $5=\frac{5}{1}$.

The rational numbers include integers, fractions and mixed numbers, terminating and repeating decimals. Every rational number can be expressed as a repeating or terminating decimal and can be shown on a number line.

Integers are positive and negative whole numbers and zero.

...-6, -5, -4, -3, -2, -1, 0, 1, 2, 3, 4, 5, 6, ...

Whole numbers are natural numbers and zero.

0, 1, 2, 3, 4, 5, 6 ...

Natural numbers are the counting numbers.

1, 2, 3, 4, 5, 6 ...

Irrational numbers are real numbers that cannot be written as the ratio of two integers. These are infinite non-repeating decimals.

Examples: $\sqrt{5} = 2.2360..$, pi $= \Pi = 3.1415927...$

A **mixed** number has an integer part and a fractional part.

Example: $2\frac{1}{4}, {}^{-}5\frac{1}{6}, 7\frac{1}{3}$

Percent = per 100 (written with the symbol %). Thus 10% $= \frac{10}{100} = \frac{1}{10}$.

Addition and Subtraction

Addition and subtraction concepts are best developed with hands-on experiences. They are taught together because they are inverse operations.

You can use objects such as apples or blocks. Addition is the "putting together" of two groups of objects and finding how many there are in all. Subtraction is the "how many are left" when you take some away.

Since addition and subtraction are inverse operations, each operation can "undo" the other. Adding 2 and 4 to get 6 is the opposite of 6 minus 4, leaving 2.

2 + 4 = 6	and	6 – 4 = 2
↓ ↓ ↓		↓
addends sum		difference

Addition and Subtraction Up to 20

Basic addition and subtraction use combinations of 1-digit numbers (3+2, 5+4, 9+6, 10-8, 19-7, etc.) and the operation of addition or subtraction.

There are basic properties of addition and subtraction that need to be understood to be successful at adding and subtracting.

Addition Properties: The Zero Property says that zero added to any number yields the original number. The Commutative Property states that the order of addends does not matter: 2 + 5 = 5 + 2.

Subtraction Rules: The Zero Property says that zero subtracted from any number yields the original number. Another rule in subtraction is that any number subtracted from itself equals zero.

Using 10 to add 9: To add 9 to any number, add 10 to that number and then subtract 1.

Finger Counting

1. **Adding**: When adding 7 + 3, students ask themselves "Open or closed?" and with addition it is open. So they open their hands and raise up 3 fingers (the smallest number). The palm of their hand is the "7" and then they continue counting on the 3 fingers to get the sum.

2. **Subtracting**: When subtracting 16 - 8, students must ask themselves "Open or closed?" With subtraction it their hand is closed. The put their hand in a fist and their palms will say the smallest number ("8"). They will count up to the higher number, which is 16. When they reach 16, they count how many fingers are up to get an answer which is 8.

Fact families: 5 + 3 = 8, 3 + 5 = 8, 8 – 5 = 3 and 8 – 3 = 5 are an example of a fact family. When you memorize fact families, it makes easier to solve problems quickly. They are also helpful when solving problems with a missing addend, such as 3 + ? = 8.

Two Digit Addition/Subtraction (No regrouping):
Place value consists of the tens and ones columns.

<u>Example:</u>

$$\begin{array}{r} \mathbf{45} \\ \underline{\mathbf{+\ 23}} \\ \mathbf{68} \end{array}$$

The problem has two columns, a ones column and a ten column.

tens	ones
4	5
+2	3
Stop	Start

Start adding/subtracting the green column (green=go) and then add/subtract the red column (red=stop).

Two Digit Addition with Regrouping:
How to move "ten" ones over to the tens column.

Example

Show the number 12 using only ones manipulatives and placing a ten manipulative in the tens column. There can be no more than 9 ones in the ones column. You need to move ten ones over into the tens column as illustrated below.

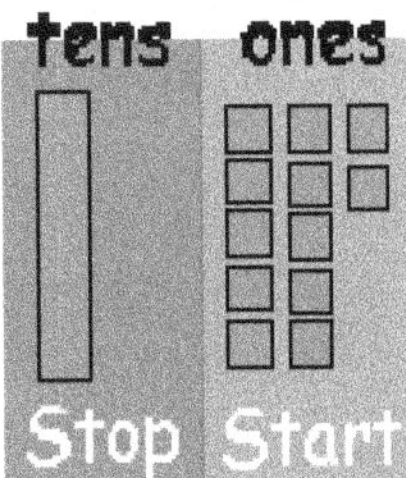

In the elementary school years, children begin to think logically but operations are still concrete and they are not able to handle abstract manipulations. This is why manipulatives are so useful in teaching basic mathematics. According to Piaget, children of this age are in the "concrete operational stage."

Children at the concrete operational stage can solve conservation tasks. The operational thought is reversible as in 3 + 4 = 4 + 3.

Two-Digit Subtraction with Regrouping: The "BBB Rule"
The BBB rules states "When the *BIG* number is on the *BOTTOM*, then you *BORROW*."

Using a place value chart offers a sure way of getting digits in the correct places. For example, to solve an addition problem, model the addends in the place value chart, regroup the blocks as needed, and then write the answer in standard form. Once these concepts are mastered, doing the problems on paper is the next challenge and the correct alignment number columns is crucial to success.

Example: At the end of a day of shopping, a shopper had $24 remaining in his wallet. He spent $45 on various goods. How much money did the shopper have at the beginning of the day?

The total amount of money the shopper started with is the sum of the amount spent and the amount remaining at the end of the day.

$$\begin{array}{r} 24 \\ +\ 45 \\ \hline 69 \end{array} \longrightarrow \text{The original total was \$69.}$$

4 hr. 8 min. 9 sec. ← Final answer

Subtraction of Whole Numbers

Example: At the end of his shift, a cashier has $96 in the cash register. At the beginning of his shift, he had $15. How much money did the cashier collect during his shift?

The total collected is the difference of the ending amount and the starting amount.

$$\begin{array}{r} 96 \\ -\ 15 \\ \hline 81 \end{array} \longrightarrow \text{The total collected was \$81.}$$

Multiplication of Whole Numbers

Multiplication is one of the four basic number operations. In simple terms, multiplication is the addition of a number to itself a certain number of times. For example, 4 multiplied by 3 is the equal to 4 + 4 + 4 or 3 + 3 + 3 +3. Another way of conceptualizing multiplication is to think in terms of groups. For example, if we have 4 groups of 3 students, the total number of students is 4 multiplied by 3. We call the solution to a multiplication problem the **product**.

The basic algorithm for whole number multiplication begins with aligning the numbers by place value with the number containing more places on top.

$$\begin{array}{r} 172 \\ \underline{\times\ \ 43} \end{array} \longrightarrow$$ Note that we placed 122 on top because it has more places than 43 does.

Next, we multiply the ones' place of the second number by each place value of the top number sequentially.

```
  (2)
  172
x  43  →   {3 x 2 = 6, 3 x 7 = 21, 3 x 1 = 3}
  516      Note that we had to carry a 2 to the hundreds' column
           because 3 x 7 = 21. Note also that we add, not
           multiply, carried numbers to the product.
```

Next, we multiply the number in the tens' place of the second number by each place value of the top number sequentially. Because we are multiplying by a number in the tens' place, we place a zero at the end of this product.

```
  (2)
  172
x  43  →   {4 x 2 = 8, 4 x 7 = 28, 4 x 1 = 4}
  516
 6880
```

Finally, to determine the final product we add the two partial products.

```
   172
x   43
   516
+ 6880
  7396  →   The product of 172 and 43 is 7396.
```

Example: A student buys 4 boxes of crayons. Each box contains 16 crayons. How many total crayons does the student have?

The total number of crayons is 16 x 4.

```
  16
 x 4  →
  64      Total number of crayons equals 64.
```

Division of Whole Numbers

Division, the inverse of multiplication, is another of the four basic number operations. When we divide one number by another, we determine how many times we can multiply the divisor (number divided by) before we exceed the number we are dividing (dividend). For example, 8 divided by 2 equals 4 because we can multiply 2 four times to reach 8 (2 x 4 = 8 or 2 + 2 + 2 + 2 = 8). Using the grouping conceptualization we used with multiplication, we can divide 8 into 4 groups of 2 or 2 groups of 4. We call the answer to a division problem the **quotient**.

If the divisor does not divide evenly into the dividend, we express the leftover amount either as a **remainder** or as a fraction with the divisor as the denominator. For example, 9 divided by 2 equals 4 with a remainder of 1 or 4 ½.

The basic algorithm for division is long division. We start by representing the quotient as follows.

$14\overline{)293}$ ⟶ 14 is the **divisor** and 293 is the **dividend.** This represents 293 ÷ 14.

Next, we divide the divisor into the dividend starting from the left.

$$\begin{array}{r} 2 \\ 14\overline{)293} \end{array}$$

⟶ 14 divides into 29 two times with a remainder.

Next, we multiply the partial quotient by the divisor, subtract this value from the first digits of the dividend, and bring down the remaining dividend digits to complete the number.

$$\begin{array}{r} 2 \\ 14\overline{)293} \\ \underline{-28} \\ 13 \end{array}$$

⟶ 2 x 14 = 28, 29 – 28 = 1, and bringing down the 3 yields 13.

Finally, we divide again (the divisor into the remaining value) and repeat the preceding process. The number left after the subtraction represents the remainder.

$$\begin{array}{r} 20 \\ 14\overline{)293} \\ \underline{-28} \\ 13 \\ \underline{-\ 0} \\ 13 \end{array}$$

⟶ The final quotient is 20 with a remainder of 13. We can also represent this quotient as 20 13/14.

Example: Each box of apples contains 24 apples. How many boxes must a grocer purchase to supply a group of 252 people with one apple each?

The grocer needs 252 apples. Because he must buy apples in groups of 24, we divide 252 by 24 to determine how many boxes he needs to buy.

```
   10
24)252
  -24
   12 ———→ The quotient is 10 with a remainder of 12.
  - 0
   12
```

Thus, the grocer needs 10 boxes plus 12 more apples. Therefore, the minimum number of boxes the grocer can purchase is 11.

Example: At his job, John gets paid $20 for every hour he works. If John made $940 in a week, how many hours did he work?

This is a division problem. To determine the number of hours John worked, we divide the total amount made ($940) by the hourly rate of pay ($20). Thus, the number of hours worked equals 940 divided by 20.

```
    47
20)940
   -80
   140
  -140
     0 ———→  20 divides into 940, 47 times with no
               remainder.
```

John worked 47 hours.

Addition and Subtraction of Decimals

When adding and subtracting decimals, we align the numbers by place value as we do with whole numbers. After adding or subtracting each column, we bring the decimal down, placing it in the same location as in the numbers added or subtracted.

Example: Find the sum of 152.3 and 36.342.

```
  152.300
+  36.342
  188.642
```

Note that we placed two zeroes after the final place value in 152.3 to clarify the column addition.

Example: Find the difference of 152.3 and 36.342.

```
      2 9 10            (4)11(12)
  152.300        →      152.300
-  36.342             -  36.342
       58               115.958
```

Note how we borrowed to subtract from the zeroes in the hundredths' and thousandths' place of 152.300.

Multiplication of Decimals

When multiplying decimal numbers, we multiply exactly as with whole numbers and place the decimal moving in from the left the total number of decimal places contained in the two numbers multiplied. For example, when multiplying 1.5 and 2.35, we place the decimal in the product 3 places in from the left (3.525).

Example: Find the product of 3.52 and 4.1.

```
    3.52 ———→  Note that there are 3 total decimal places
  x  4.1       in the two numbers.
    352
+ 14080
  14432 ———→   We place the decimal 3 places in from the
               left.
```

Thus, the final product is 14.432.

Example: A shopper has 5 one-dollar bills, 6 quarters, 3 nickels, and 4 pennies in his pocket. How much money does he have?

```
                        3
5 x $1.00 = $5.00   $0.25    $0.05    $0.01
                    x   6    x   3    x   4
                    $1.50    $0.15    $0.04
```

Note the placement of the decimals in the multiplication products. Thus, the total amount of money in the shopper's pocket is:

```
  $5.00
   1.50
   0.15
+  0.04
  $6.69
```

Division of Decimals

When dividing decimal numbers, we first remove the decimal in the divisor by moving the decimal in the dividend the same number of spaces to the right. For example, when dividing 1.45 into 5.3 we convert the numbers to 145 and 530 and perform normal whole number division.

Example: Find the quotient of 5.3 divided by 1.45.
Convert to 145 and 530.

Divide.

$$\begin{array}{r} 3 \\ 145\overline{)530} \\ -435 \\ \hline 95 \end{array} \longrightarrow \begin{array}{r} 3.65 \\ 145\overline{)530.00} \\ -435 \\ \hline 950 \\ -870 \\ \hline 800 \end{array}$$

→ Note that we insert the decimal to continue division.

Because one of the numbers divided contained one decimal place, we round the quotient to one decimal place. Thus, the final quotient is 3.7.

Addition and Subtraction of Fractions

Key Points

1. You need a common denominator in order to add and subtract reduced and improper fractions.

Example: $\frac{1}{3}+\frac{7}{3}=\frac{1+7}{3}=\frac{8}{3}=2\frac{2}{3}$

Example: $\frac{4}{12}+\frac{6}{12}-\frac{3}{12}=\frac{4+6-3}{12}=\frac{7}{12}$

2. Adding an integer and a fraction of the <u>same</u> sign results directly in a mixed fraction.

Example: $2+\frac{2}{3}=2\frac{2}{3}$

Example: ${}^{-}2-\frac{3}{4}={}^{-}2\frac{3}{4}$

3. Adding an integer and a fraction with different signs involves the following steps.

-get a common denominator
-add or subtract as needed
-change to a mixed fraction if possible

Example: $2-\frac{1}{3}=\frac{2\times 3-1}{3}=\frac{6-1}{3}=\frac{5}{3}=1\frac{2}{3}$

Example: Add $7\frac{3}{8}+5\frac{2}{7}$

Add the whole numbers; add the fractions and combine the two results:

$$7\frac{3}{8}+5\frac{2}{7}=(7+5)+(\frac{3}{8}+\frac{2}{7})$$

$$=12+\frac{(7\times 3)+(8\times 2)}{56} \quad \text{(LCM of 8 and 7)}$$

$$=12+\frac{21+16}{56}=12+\frac{37}{56}=12\frac{37}{56}$$

Example: Perform the operation.

$$\frac{2}{3}-\frac{5}{6}$$

We first find the LCM of 3 and 6 which is 6.

$$\frac{2\times 2}{3\times 2}-\frac{5}{6}\rightarrow\frac{4-5}{6}=\frac{^-1}{6} \quad \text{(Using method A)}$$

Example: $^-7\frac{1}{4}+2\frac{7}{8}$

$$^-7\frac{1}{4}+2\frac{7}{8}=(^-7+2)+(\frac{^-1}{4}+\frac{7}{8})$$

$$=(^-5)+\frac{(^-2+7)}{8}=(^-5)+(\frac{5}{8})$$

$$=(^-5)+\frac{5}{8}=\frac{^-5\times 8}{1\times 8}+\frac{5}{8}=\frac{^-40+5}{8}$$

$$=\frac{^-35}{8}={}^-4\frac{3}{8}$$

Divide 35 by 8 to get 4, remainder 3.

Caution: Common error would be

$$^{-}7\frac{1}{4}+2\frac{7}{8}={}^{-}7\frac{2}{8}+2\frac{7}{8}={}^{-}5\frac{9}{8}$$ Wrong.

It is correct to add -7 and 2 to get -5, but adding $\frac{2}{8}+\frac{7}{8}=\frac{9}{8}$ is wrong. It should have been $\frac{^{-}2}{8}+\frac{7}{8}=\frac{5}{8}$. Then, $^{-}5+\frac{5}{8}={}^{-}4\frac{3}{8}$ as before.

Multiplication of Fractions

Using the following example: $3\frac{1}{4}\times\frac{5}{6}$

1. Convert each number to an improper fraction.

$3\frac{1}{4}=\frac{(12+1)}{4}=\frac{13}{4}$ $\frac{5}{6}$ is already in reduced form.

2. Reduce (cancel) common factors of the numerator and denominator if they exist.

$\frac{13}{4}\times\frac{5}{6}$ No common factors exist.

3. Multiply the numerators by each other and the denominators by each other.

$$\frac{13}{4}\times\frac{5}{6}=\frac{65}{24}$$

4. If possible, reduce the fraction back to its lowest term.

$\frac{65}{24}$ Cannot be reduced further.

5. Convert the improper fraction back to a mixed fraction by using long division.

$$\frac{65}{24} = 24\overline{)65}^{\,2} \qquad \begin{array}{r} 48 \\ \hline 17 \end{array} \qquad = 2\frac{17}{24}$$

Summary of Sign Changes for Multiplication

a. $(+)\times(+)=(+)$

b. $(-)\times(+)=(-)$

c. $(+)\times(-)=(-)$

d. $(-)\times(-)=(+)$

Example: $7\frac{1}{3}\times\frac{5}{11}=\frac{22}{3}\times\frac{5}{11}$ Reduce like terms (22 and 11)

$$=\frac{2}{3}\times\frac{5}{1}=\frac{10}{3}=3\frac{1}{3}$$

Example: $^{-}6\frac{1}{4}\times\frac{5}{9}=\frac{^{-}25}{4}\times\frac{5}{9}$

$$=\frac{^{-}125}{36}={}^{-}3\frac{17}{36}$$

Example: $\frac{^{-}1}{4}\times\frac{^{-}3}{7}$ Negative times a negative equals positive.

$$=\frac{1}{4}\times\frac{3}{7}=\frac{3}{28}$$

Division of Fractions

1. Change mixed fractions to improper fraction.
2. Change the division problem to a multiplication problem by using the reciprocal of the number after the division sign.

3. Find the sign of the final product.

4. Cancel if common factors exist between the numerator and the denominator.

5. Multiply the numerators together and the denominators together.

6. Change the improper fraction to a mixed number.

Example: $3\frac{1}{5} \div 2\frac{1}{4} = \frac{16}{5} \div \frac{9}{4}$

$= \frac{16}{5} \times \frac{4}{9}$ Reciprocal of $\frac{9}{4}$ is $\frac{4}{9}$.

$= \frac{64}{45} = 1\frac{19}{45}$

Example: $7\frac{3}{4} \div 11\frac{5}{8} = \frac{31}{4} \div \frac{93}{8}$

$= \frac{31}{4} \times \frac{8}{93}$ Reduce like terms.

$= \frac{1}{1} \times \frac{2}{3} = \frac{2}{3}$

Example: $\left(^{-}2\frac{1}{2}\right) \div 4\frac{1}{6} = \frac{^{-}5}{2} \div \frac{25}{6}$

$= \frac{^{-}5}{2} \times \frac{6}{25}$ Reduce like terms.

$= \frac{^{-}1}{1} \times \frac{3}{5} = \frac{^{-}3}{5}$

Example: $\left(^{-}5\frac{3}{8}\right)\div\left(\frac{^{-}7}{16}\right)=\frac{^{-}43}{8}\div\frac{^{-}7}{16}$

$=\frac{^{-}43}{8}\times\frac{^{-}16}{7}$ Reduce like terms.

$=\frac{43}{1}\times\frac{2}{7}$ Negative times a negative equals a positive.

$=\frac{86}{7}=12\frac{2}{7}$

Skill 7.2 Demonstrate knowledge of the correct order of operations

The **order of operations** is to be followed when evaluating algebraic expressions. Follow these steps in order:

1. Simplify inside grouping characters such as parentheses, brackets, square root, fraction bar, etc.
2. Multiply out expressions with exponents.
3. Do multiplication or division, from left to right.
4. Do addition or subtraction, from left to right.

Example: $3^3-5(b+2)$

$=3^3-5b-10$

$=27-5b-10=17-5b$

Example: $2-4\times2^3-2(4-2\times3)$

$=2-4\times2^3-2(4-6)=2-4\times2^3-2(^{-}2)$

According to the Order of Operations, PEMDAS, parentheses are dealt with first, then exponents, then multiplication or division and finally addition and subtraction (whichever comes first, go from left to right).

Skill 7.3 Recognize and interpreting mathematical symbols (e.g., +, –, <, >, ≤, ≥)

Symbol for inequality: In the symbol '>' (greater than) or '<' (less than), the big open side of the symbol always faces the larger of the two numbers and the point of the symbol always faces the smaller number.

Example: Compare 15 and 20 on the number line.

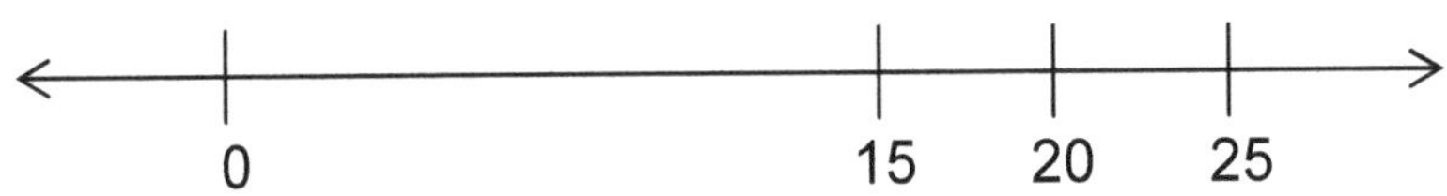

Since 20 is further away from the zero than 15 is, then 20 is greater than 15, or $20 > 15$.

Example: Compare $\frac{3}{7}$ and $\frac{5}{10}$.

To compare fractions, they should have the same least common denominator (LCD). The LCD in this example is 70.

$$\frac{3}{7} = \frac{3 \times 10}{7 \times 10} = \frac{30}{70} \qquad \frac{5}{10} = \frac{5 \times 7}{10 \times 7} = \frac{35}{70}$$

Since the denominators are equal, compare only the denominators. $30 < 35$, so:

$$\frac{3}{7} < \frac{5}{10}$$

Skill 7.4 Demonstrate knowledge of definitions of basic terms such as sum, difference, product, quotient, numerator, and denominator

Sum: The result of adding two numbers.

For example: 12 + 6 = 18

Difference: The result of subtracting two numbers.

For example: 57 – 29 = 28

Product: The result of two numbers being multiplied together.

For example: 5 x 5 = 25

Quotient: The result of dividing one number by another.

For example: 32 / 8 = 4

Numerator: The number above the bar in a fraction that tells how many equal parts of the whole are being considered

Denominator: The number below the bar in a fraction that tells how many equal parts are in the whole

For example: $\frac{3}{4}$ ← Numerator / ← Denominator

Skill 7.5 Recognize the relative positions of numbers on a number line (e.g., 13 is between 14 and 12) and equivalent forms of numbers (e.g., 12= .5)

See Skill 7.3.

Skill 7.6 Demonstrate knowledge of place value for whole numbers and decimal numbers

Whole Number Place Value

Consider the number 792. We can assign a place value to each digit.

Reading from left to right, the first digit (7) represents the hundreds' place. The hundreds' place tells us how many sets of one hundred the number contains. Thus, there are 7 sets of one hundred in the number 792.

The second digit (9) represents the tens' place. The tens' place tells us how many sets of ten the number contains. Thus, there are 9 sets of ten in the number 792.

The last digit (2) represents the ones' place. The ones' place tells us how many ones the number contains. Thus, there are 2 sets of one in the number 792.

Therefore, there are 7 sets of 100, plus 9 sets of 10, plus 2 ones in the number 792.

Decimal Place Value

More complex numbers have additional place values to both the left and right of the decimal point. Consider the number 374.8.

Reading from left to right, the first digit (3) is in the hundreds' place and tells us the number contains 3 sets of one hundred.

The second digit (7) is in the tens' place and tells us the number contains 7 sets of ten.

The third digit, 4, is in the ones' place and tells us the number contains 4 ones.

Finally, the number after the decimal (8) is in the tenths' place and tells us the number contains 8 tenths.

Skill 7.7 Demonstrate the ability to solve problems (e.g., basic math operations and/or estimation)

To estimate measurement of familiar objects, it is first necessary to determine the units to be used.

<u>Examples:</u>
Length
1. The coastline of Florida
2. The width of a ribbon
3. The thickness of a book
4. The depth of water in a pool

Weight or mass
1. A bag of sugar
2. A school bus
3. A dime

Capacity or volume
1. Paint to paint a bedroom
2. Glass of milk

Money
1. Cost of a house
2. Cost of a cup of coffee
3. Exchange rate

Perimeter
1. The edge of a backyard
2. The edge of a football field

Area
1. The size of a carpet
2. The size of a state

Example: Estimate the measurements of the following objects:

Length of a dollar bill	6 inches
Weight of a baseball	1 pound
Distance from New York to Florida	1100 km
Volume of water to fill a medicine dropper	1 milliliter
Length of a desk	2 meters
Temperature of water in a swimming pool	80° F

Depending on the degree of accuracy needed, an object may be measured to different units. For example, a pencil may be 6 inches to the nearest inch, or 6 3/8 inches to the nearest eighth of an inch. Similarly, it might be 15 cm to the nearest cm or 154 mm to the nearest mm.

Given a set of objects and their measurements, the use of rounding procedures is helpful when attempting to round to the nearest given unit. When rounding to a given place value, it is necessary to look at the number in the next smaller place. If this number is 5 or more, the number in the place we are rounding to is increased by one and all numbers to the right are changed to zero. If the number is less than 5, the number in the place we are rounding to stays the same and all numbers to the right are changed to zero.

One method of rounding measurements can require an additional step. First, the measurement must be converted to a decimal number. Then the rules for rounding applied.

Example: Round the measurements to the given units.

MEASUREMENT	ROUND TO NEAREST	ANSWER
1 foot 7 inches	foot	2 ft
5 pound 6 ounces	pound	5 pounds
$5\ ^{9}/_{16}$ inches	inch	6 inches

Convert each measurement to a decimal number. Then apply the rules for rounding.

1 foot 7 inches = $1\frac{7}{12}$ ft = 1.58333 ft, round up to 2 ft

5 pounds 6 ounces = $5\frac{6}{16}$ pounds = 5.375 pound, round to 5 pounds

$5\frac{9}{16}$ inches = 5.5625 inches, round up to 6 inches

Example: Janet goes into a store to purchase a CD on sale for $13.95. While shopping, she sees two pairs of shoes, prices $19.95 and $14.50. She only has $50. Can she purchase everything?

Solve by rounding:

$19.95→$20.00
$14.50→$15.00
$13.95→$14.00
$49.00 Yes, she can purchase the CD and the shoes.

Skill 7.8 Demonstrate the ability to solve a single-step equation involving one variable (e.g., find *x* if *x* + 3 = 5)

Procedure for Solving Algebraic Equations

Example: $3(x+3) = {}^{-}2x+4$ Solve for x.

1. Expand to eliminate all parentheses.
   $3x+9 = {}^{-}2x+4$

2. Multiply each term by the LCD to eliminate all denominators.

3. Combine like terms on each side when possible.

4. Use the properties to put all variables on one side and all constants on the other side.

$\rightarrow 3x+9-9 = {}^{-}2x+4-9$ (subtract nine from both sides)

$\rightarrow 3x = {}^{-}2x-5$

$\rightarrow 3x+2x = {}^{-}2x+2x-5$ (add $2x$ to both sides)

$\rightarrow 5x = {}^{-}5$

$\rightarrow \frac{5x}{5} = \frac{{}^{-}5}{5}$ (divide both sides by 5)

$\rightarrow x = {}^{-}1$

Example: Solve: $3(2x+5)-4x=5(x+9)$

$$6x+15-4x=5x+45$$
$$2x+15=5x+45$$
$$^{-}3x+15=45$$
$$^{-}3x=30$$
$$x={}^{-}10$$

Example: Mark and Mike are twins. Three times Mark's age plus four equals four times Mike's age minus 14. How old are the boys?

Since the boys are twins, their ages are the same. "Translate" the English into Algebra. Let x = their age

$3x + 4 = 4x - 14$

$18 = x$

The boys are each 18 years old.

Example: The YMCA wants to sell raffle tickets to raise $32,000. If they must pay $7,250 in expenses and prizes out of the money collected from the tickets, how many tickets worth $25 each must they sell?

Let $x =$ number of tickets sold
Then $25x =$ total money collected for x tickets

Total money minus expenses is greater than $32,000.

$25x - 7250 = 32,000$
$25x = 39350$
$x = 1570$

If they sell 1,570 tickets, they will raise $32,000.

Example: The Simpsons went out for dinner. All 4 of them ordered the aardvark steak dinner. Bert paid for the 4 meals and included a tip of $12 for a total of $84.60. How much was an aardvark steak dinner?

Let $x =$ the price of one aardvark dinner.
So $4x =$ the price of 4 aardvark dinners.

Skill 7.9 Demonstrate the ability to compute percentages

Percent means per 100 (%).

Example: 10 percent $= \frac{10}{100} = \frac{1}{10} = 0.1$

Example: 10 percent of 150 means $\frac{10}{100} \times \frac{150}{1} = 15$

Example: Add 75% of 25 to 10% of 1000.

75% of 25 $= \frac{75}{100} \times \frac{25}{1} = \frac{75}{4} \times \frac{1}{1} = \frac{75}{4} = 18\frac{3}{4}$ and

10% of 1000 $= \frac{10}{100} \times \frac{1000}{1} = \frac{10}{1} \times \frac{10}{1} = 100$

Adding the two numbers gives:

$18\frac{3}{4} + 100 = 118\frac{3}{4}$ or 118.75

Example: 5 is what percent of 20?

This is the same as converting $\frac{5}{20}$ to % form.

$\frac{5}{20} \times \frac{100}{1} = \frac{5}{1} \times \frac{5}{1} = 25\%$

Example: An item on sale at 75% discount is now sold for $12.50. What was the selling price before the sale?

$12.50 is 75% of the price. What was full price?

$\frac{12.50}{75} \times \frac{100}{1} = \frac{50}{3} = \$16.667 \approx \$16.67$

Example: There are 64 dogs in the kennel. 48 are collies. What percent are collies?

Restate the problem.	48 is what percent of 64?
Write an equation.	$48 = n \times 64$
Solve.	$\frac{48}{64} = n$

$n = \frac{3}{4} = 75\%$

75% of the dogs are collies.

Example: The auditorium was filled to 90% capacity. There were 558 seats occupied. What is the capacity of the auditorium?

Restate the problem.	90% of what number is 558?
Write an equation.	$0.9n = 558$
Solve.	$n = \frac{558}{.9}$
	$n = 620$

The capacity of the auditorium is 620 people.

Example: A pair of shoes costs \$42.00. Sales tax is 6%. What is the total cost of the shoes?

Restate the problem.	What is 6% of 42?
Write an equation.	$n = 0.06 \times 42$
Solve.	$n = 2.52$

Add the sales tax to the cost. \$42.00 + \$2.52 = \$44.52

The total cost of the shoes, including sales tax, is \$44.52.

www.nctm.org

COMPETENCY 8.0 UNDERSTAND BASIC CONCEPTS OF GEOMETRY AND MEASUREMENT

Skill 8.1 Demonstrate the ability to represent time and money in more than one way (e.g., 15 minutes = 1/4 hour; 10:45 = quarter of eleven; $.25 = a quarter)

Elapsed **time** problems are usually one of two types. One type of problem is the elapsed time between two times given in hours, minutes, and seconds. The other common type of problem is between two times given in months and years.

For any time of day past noon, change it into military time by adding 12 hours. For instance, 1:15 p.m. would be 13:15. Remember when you borrow a minute or an hour in a subtraction problem that you have borrowed 60 more seconds or minutes.

Example: Find the time from 11:34:22 a.m. until 3:28:40 p.m.

First change 3:28:40 p.m. to 15:28:40 p.m.
Now subtract - 11:34:22 a.m.
:18

Borrow an hour and add 60 more minutes. Subtract
14:88:40 p.m.
- 11:34:22 a.m.
3:54:18 ↔ 3 hours, 54 minutes, 18 seconds

Example: A race took the winner 1 hr. 58 min. 12 sec. on the first half of the race and 2 hr. 9 min. 57 sec. on the second half of the race. How much time did the entire race take?

1 hr. 58 min. 12 sec.
+ 2 hr. 9 min. 57 sec. Add these numbers
3 hr. 67 min. 69 sec
+ 1 min = 60 sec. Change 60 seconds to 1 min.
3 hr. 68 min. 9 sec.
+ 1 hr. = 60 min. Change 60 minutes to 1 hr.
4 hr. 8 min. 9 sec. ← final answer

Example: It takes Cynthia 45 minutes to get ready each morning. How many hours does she spend getting ready each week?

45 minutes X 7 days = 315 minutes

$$\frac{\text{315 minutes}}{\text{60 minutes in an hour}} = \text{5.25 hours}$$

Money

Example: Juan earned $75 for mowing lawns one weekend. He needs to replenish his supplies by buying 2 gallons of gas $3.50 a gallon, a new hedge clipper for $35.00, and a box of trash bags for $4.50. What is Juan's profit?

2 gallons of gas x $3.50 per gallon	$7.00
Hedge clipper	35.00
Trash bags	4.50
Cost of purchases	$46.50

Money earned	$75.00
Less purchases	-46.50
Profit	$28.50

Weight

Example: The weight limit of a playground merry-go-round is 1000 pounds. There are 11 children on the merry-go-round.
3 children weigh 100 pounds.
6 children weigh 75 pounds
2 children weigh 60 pounds

George weighs 80 pounds. Can he get on the merry-go-round?

3(100) + 6(75) + 2(60)
= 300 + 450 + 120
= 870
1000 – 870
= 130

Since 80 is less than 130, George can get on the merry-go-round.

Skill 8.2 Recognize techniques for converting between units of length, mass, volume, and weight in the same measurement system (e.g., feet to yards, milliliters to liters)

Measurements of length (English system)

12 inches (in)	=	1 foot (ft)
3 feet (ft)	=	1 yard (yd)
1760 yards (yd)	=	1 mile (mi)

Measurements of length (metric system)

kilometer (km)	=	1000 meters (m)
hectometer (hm)	=	100 meters (m)
decameter (dam)	=	10 meters (m)
meter (m)	=	1 meter (m)
decimeter (dm)	=	1/10 meter (m)
centimeter (cm)	=	1/100 meter (m)
millimeter (mm)	=	1/1000 meter (m)

Conversion of length from English to metric

1 inch	=	2.54 centimeters
1 foot	≈	30 centimeters
1 yard	≈	0.9 meters
1 mile	≈	1.6 kilometers

Measurements of weight (English system)

28 grams (g)	=	1 ounce (oz)
16 ounces (oz)	=	1 pound (lb)
2000 pounds (lb)	=	1 ton (t)(short ton)
1.1 ton (t)	=	1 ton (t)

Measurements of weight (metric system)

kilogram (kg)	=	1000 grams (g)
gram (g)	=	1 gram (g)
milligram (mg)	=	1/1000 gram (g)

Conversion of weight from English to metric

1 ounce	≈	28 grams
1 pound	≈	0.45 kilogram
	≈	454 grams

Measurement of volume (English system)

8 fluid ounces (oz)	=	1 cup C.
2 cups C.	=	1 pint (pt)
2 pints (pt)	=	1 quart (qt)
4 quarts (qt)	=	1 gallon (gal)

Measurement of volume (metric system)

kiloliter (kl)	=	1000 liters (l)
liter (l)	=	1 liter (l)
milliliter (ml)	=	1/1000 liters (ml)

Conversion of volume from English to metric

1 teaspoon (tsp)	≈	5 milliliters
1 fluid ounce	≈	15 milliliters
1 cup	≈	0.24 liters
1 pint	≈	0.47 liters
1 quart	≈	0.95 liters
1 gallon	≈	3.8 liters

Measurement of time

1 second	=	
1 minute	=	60 seconds
1 hour	=	60 minutes
1 day	=	24 hours
1 week	=	7 days
1 year	=	365 days
1 century	=	100 years

Note: (’) represents feet and (”) represents inches.

Skill 8.3 Identify basic geometric figures (e.g., right triangle, cylinder, polygon)

Polygons, simple closed **two-dimensional figures** composed of line segments, are named according to the number of sides they have.

A **quadrilateral** is a polygon with four sides.
The sum of the measures of the angles of a quadrilateral is 360°.

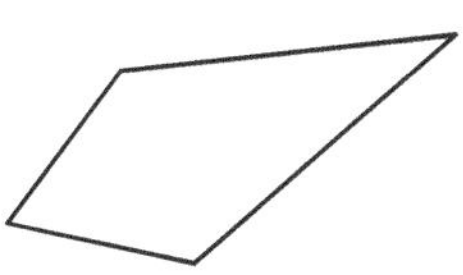

A **trapezoid** is a quadrilateral with exactly one pair of parallel sides.

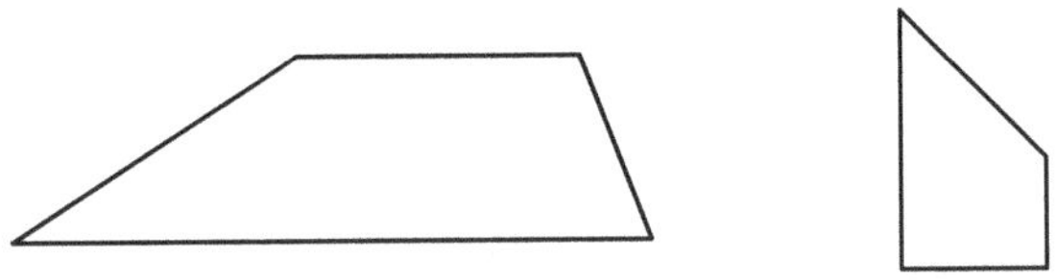

In an **isosceles trapezoid**, the non-parallel sides are congruent.

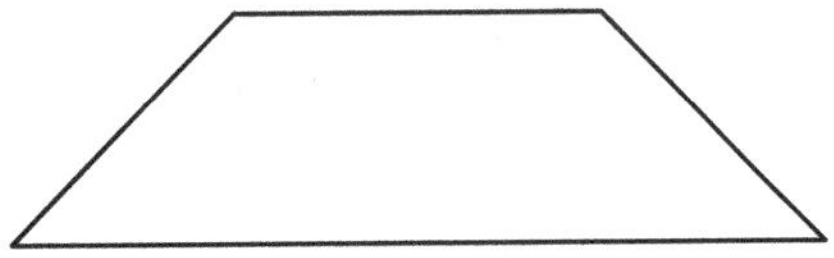

A **parallelogram** is a quadrilateral with two pairs of parallel sides.

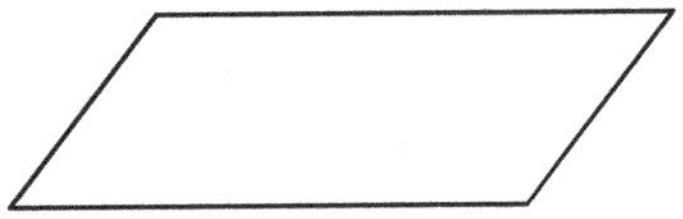

In a parallelogram:

- The diagonals bisect each other.
- Each diagonal divides the parallelogram into two congruent triangles.
- Both pairs of opposite sides are congruent.
- Both pairs of opposite angles are congruent.
- Two adjacent angles are supplementary.

A **rectangle** is a parallelogram with a right angle.

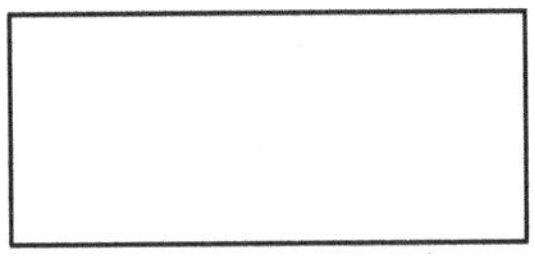

A **rhombus** is a parallelogram with all sides equal length.

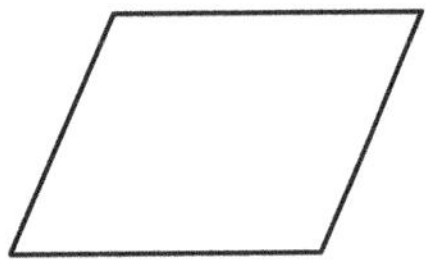

A **square** is a rectangle with all sides equal length.

Example: True or false?

All squares are rhombuses.	True
All parallelograms are rectangles.	False - some parallelograms are rectangles
All rectangles are parallelograms.	True
Some rhombuses are squares.	True
Some rectangles are trapezoids.	False - only one pair of parallel sides
All quadrilaterals are parallelograms.	False -some quadrilaterals are parallelograms
Some squares are rectangles.	False - all squares are rectangles
Some parallelograms are rhombuses.	True

A **triangle** is a polygon with three sides.

Triangles can be classified by the types of angles or the lengths of their sides.

An **acute** triangle has exactly three *acute* angles.
A **right** triangle has one *right* angle.
An **obtuse** triangle has one *obtuse* angle.

acute   right   obtuse

For Lesson Plans and Teaching Materials,
Visit the Geometry Junkyard at
http://www.ics.uci.edu/~eppstein/junkyard/teach.html

All *three* sides of an **equilateral** triangle are the same length.
Two sides of an **isosceles** triangle are the same length.
None of the sides of a **scalene** triangle are the same length.

equilateral

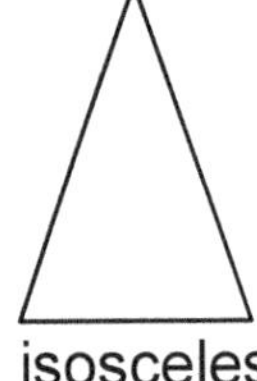
isosceles

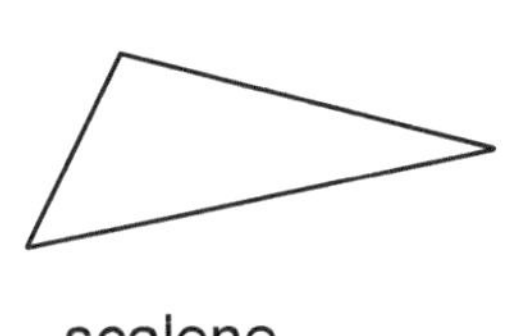
scalene

Example: Can a triangle have two right angles?
No. A right angle measures 90°; therefore the sum of two right angles would be 180° and there could not be third angle.

Example: Can a triangle have two obtuse angles?
No. Since an obtuse angle measures more than 90° the sum of two obtuse angles would be greater than 180°.

A **cylinder** has two congruent circular bases that are parallel.

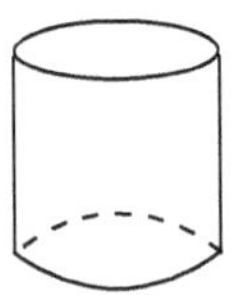

A **sphere** is a space figure having all its points the same distance from the center.

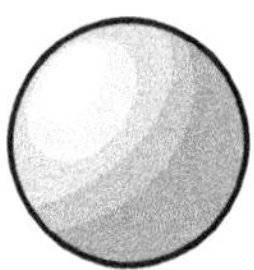

A **cone** is a space figure having a circular base and a single vertex.

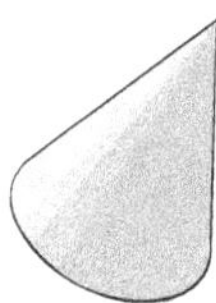

A **pyramid** is a space figure with a square base and 4 triangle-shaped sides.

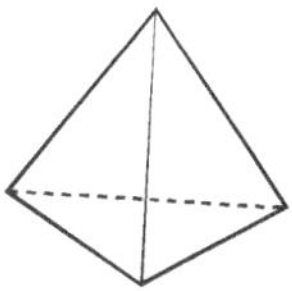

A **tetrahedron** is a 4-sided space triangle. Each face is a triangle.

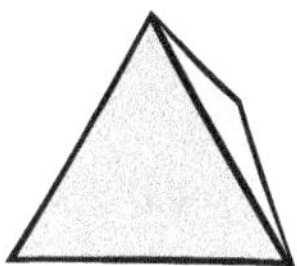

A **prism** is a space figure with two congruent, parallel bases that are polygons.

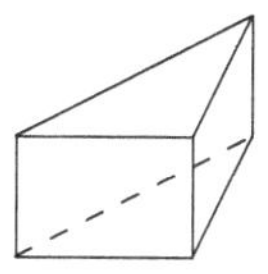

Skill 8.4 Demonstrate the ability to perform basic computations related to area, volume, and perimeter for basic geometric figures

The **perimeter** of any polygon is the sum of the lengths of the sides.

The **area** of a polygon is the number of square units covered by the figure.

FIGURE	AREA FORMULA	PERIMETER FORMULA
Rectangle	LW	$2(L+W)$
Triangle	$\frac{1}{2}bh$	$a+b+c$
Parallelogram	bh	sum of lengths of sides
Trapezoid	$\frac{1}{2}h(a+b)$	sum of lengths of sides

Perimeter

Example: A farmer has a piece of land shaped as shown below. He wishes to fence this land at an estimated cost of $25 per linear foot. What is the total cost of fencing this property to the nearest foot?

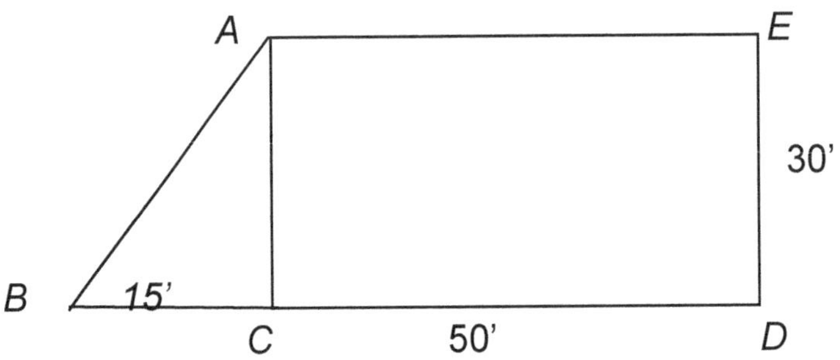

From the right triangle ABC, AC = 30 and BC = 15.

Since $(AB) = (AC)^2 + (BC)^2$
$(AB) = (30)^2 + (15)^2$

So $\sqrt{(AB)^2} = AB = \sqrt{1125} = 33.5410$ feet
To the nearest foot AB = 34 feet.

Perimeter of the piece of land is $= AB + BC + CD + DE + EA$
= 34 + 15 + 50 + 30 + 50 = 179 feet

cost of fencing = $25 x 179 = $4, 475.00

Area is the space that a figure occupies. Example:

Example: What will be the cost of carpeting a rectangular office that measures 12 feet by 15 feet if the carpet costs $12.50 per square yard?

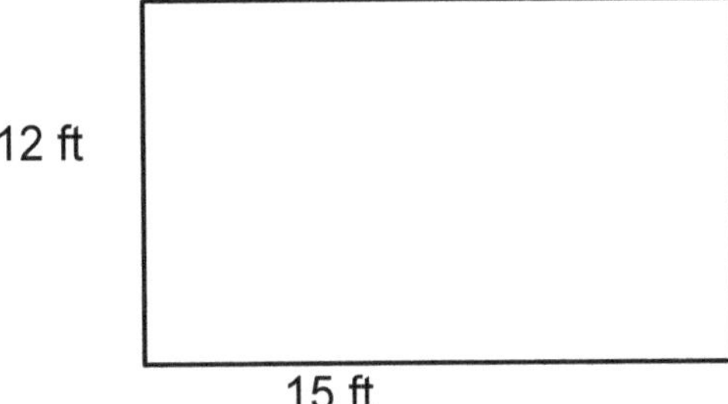

The problem is asking you to determine the area of the office. The area of a rectangle is *length x width = A*
Substitute the given values in the equation *A = lw*

A = (12 ft.)(15 ft.)
A = 180 ft.

The problem asked you to determine the cost of carpet at $12.50 per square yard.

First, you need to convert 180 ft.^{2} into yards^2.

$$1 \text{ yd.} = 3 \text{ ft.}$$
$$(1 \text{ yard})(1 \text{ yard}) = (3 \text{ feet})(3 \text{ feet})$$
$$1 \text{ yd}^2 = 9 \text{ ft } 2$$

Hence, $\frac{180 \text{ ft}^2}{1} = \frac{1 \text{ yd}^2}{9 \text{ ft}^2} = \frac{20}{1} = 20 \text{ yd}^2$

The carpet cost $12.50 per square yard; thus the cost of carpeting the office described is $12.50 x 20 = $250.00.

Example: Find the area of a parallelogram whose base is 6.5 cm and the height of the altitude to that base is 3.7 cm.

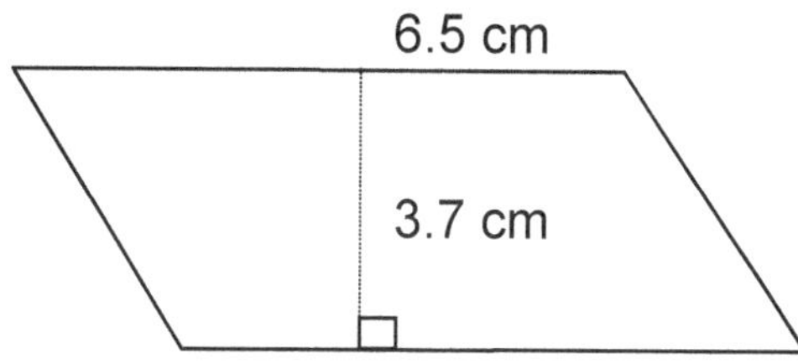

$$A_{parallelogram} = bh$$
$$= (3.7)(6.5)$$
$$= 24.05 \text{ cm}^2$$

Example: Find the area of this triangle.

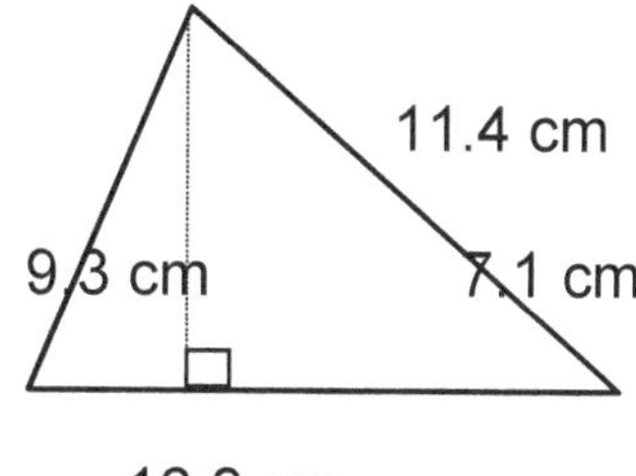

$$A_{triangle} = \tfrac{1}{2}bh$$
$$= 0.5\,(16.8)\,(7.1)$$
$$= 59.64 \text{ cm}^2$$

Example: Find the area of this trapezoid.

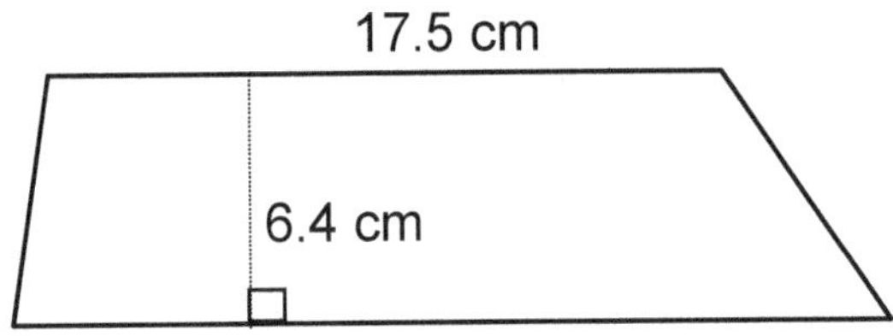

23.7 cm

The area of a trapezoid equals one-half the sum of the bases times the altitude.

$$
\begin{aligned}
A_{trapezoid} &= \tfrac{1}{2}h(b_1 + b_2) \\
&= 0.5\,(6.4)\,(17.5 + 23.7) \\
&= 131.84\ \text{cm}^2
\end{aligned}
$$

The distance around a circle is the **circumference**. The ratio of the circumference to the diameter is represented by the Greek letter pi. $\Pi \sim 3.14 \sim \frac{22}{7}$.

The circumference of a circle is found by the formula $C = 2\Pi r$ or $C = \Pi d$ where r is the radius of the circle and d is the diameter.

The **area** of a circle is found by the formula $A = \Pi r^2$.

Example: Find the circumference and area of a circle whose radius is 7 meters.

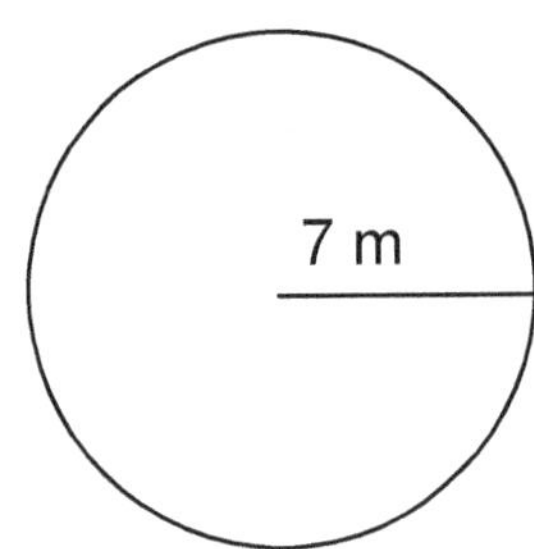

$C = 2\Pi r$
$= 2(3.14)(7)$
$= 43.96$ m

$A = \Pi r^2$
$= 3.14(7)(7)$
$= 153.86\ \text{m}^2$

COMPETENCY 9.0 UNDERSTAND CONCEPTS RELATED TO DATA ANALYSIS

Skill 9.1 Demonstrate the ability to interpret and/or compare information from tables, charts, and graphs

Using visuals to supplement writing and to depict complex data is an excellent way to increase comprehension. Students must be able to analyze the information in these tables, charts, and graphs to grasp the significant relationships.

To make a **bar graph** or a **pictograph**, determine the scale to be used for the graph. Then determine the length of each bar on the graph or determine the number of pictures needed to represent each item of information. Be sure to include an explanation of the scale in the legend.

Example: A class had the following grades: 4 A's, 9 B's, 8 C's, 1 D, 3 F's. Graph these on a bar graph and a pictograph.

Pictograph

Grade	Number of Students
A	☺☺☺☺
B	☺☺☺☺☺☺☺☺☺
C	☺☺☺☺☺☺☺☺
D	☺
F	☺☺☺

Bar graph

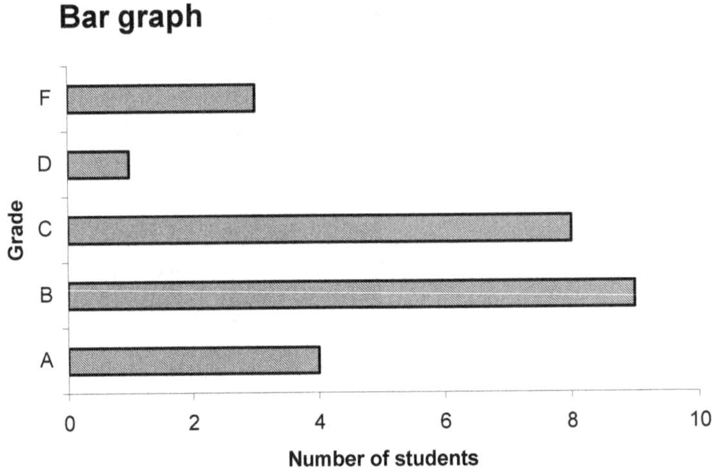

To make a **line graph**, determine appropriate scales for both the vertical and horizontal axes (based on the information to be graphed). Describe what each axis represents and mark the scale periodically on each axis. Graph the individual points of the graph and connect the points on the graph from left to right.

Example: Graph the following information using a line graph.

The number of National Merit finalists/school year

	90-91	91-92	92-93	93-94	94-95	95-96
Central	3	5	1	4	6	8
Wilson	4	2	3	2	3	2

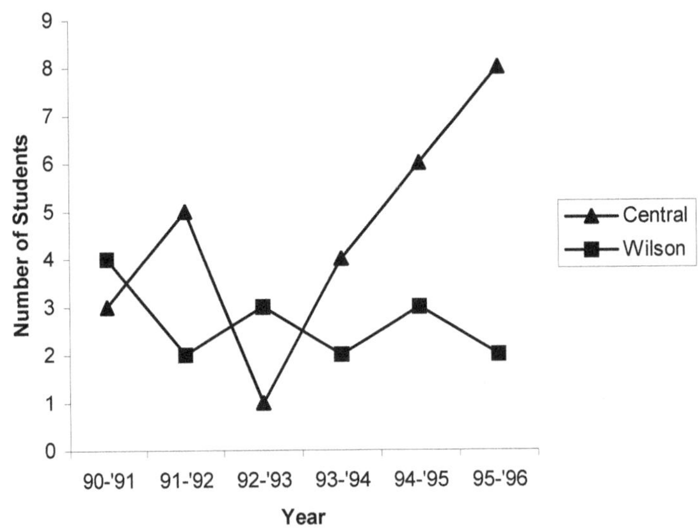

To make a **circle graph**, total all the information that is to be included on the graph. Determine the central angle to be used for each sector of the graph using the following formula:

$$\frac{\text{information}}{\text{total information}} \times 360^\circ = \text{degrees in central} \measuredangle$$

Lay out the central angles to these sizes, label each section and include its percent.

Example: Graph this information on a circle graph:

Monthly expenses:

(a) Rent, $400
Food, $150
Utilities, $75
Clothes, $75
Church, $100
Misc., $200

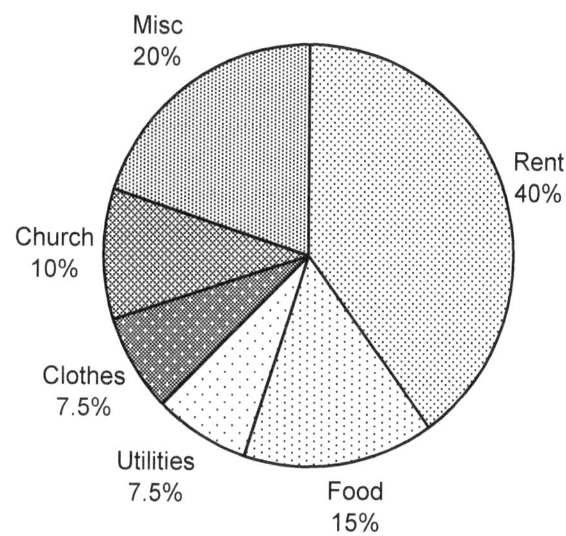

Scatter plots compare two characteristics of the same group of things or people and usually consist of a large body of data. They show how much one variable is affected by another. The relationship between the two variables is their **correlation**. The closer the data points come to making a straight line when plotted, the closer the correlation.

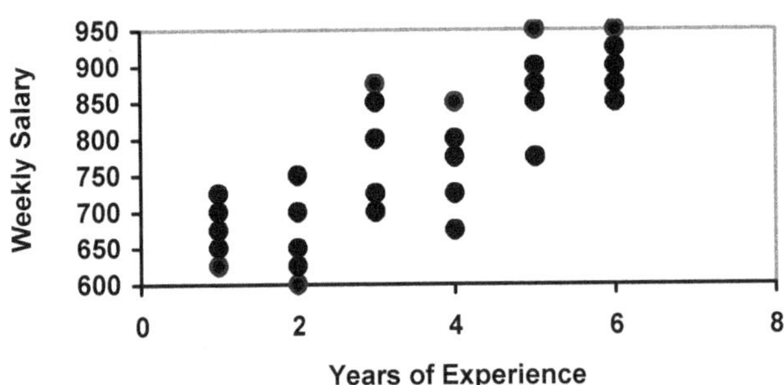

Stem and leaf plots are visually similar to line plots. The **stems** are the digits in the greatest place value of the data values, and the **leaves** are the digits in the next greatest place values. Stem and leaf plots are best suited for small sets of data and are especially useful for comparing two sets of data. The following is an example using test scores:

4	9
5	4 9
6	1 2 3 4 6 7 8 8
7	0 3 4 6 6 6 7 7 7 7 8 8 8 8
8	3 5 5 7 8
9	0 0 3 4 5
10	0 0

Histograms are used to summarize information from large sets of data that can be naturally grouped into intervals. The vertical axis indicates **frequency** (the number of times any particular data value occurs), and the horizontal axis indicates data values or ranges of data values. The number of data values in any interval is the **frequency of the interval**.

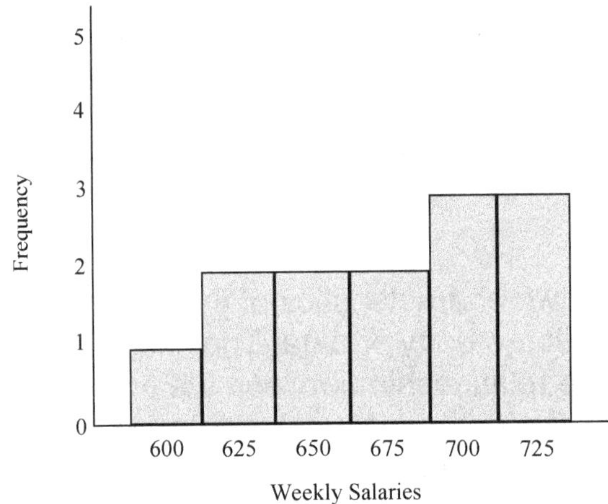

A **trend** line on a line graph shows the correlation between two sets of data. A trend may show positive correlation (both sets of data get bigger together), negative correlation (one set of data gets bigger while the other gets smaller), or no correlation.

An **inference** is a statement which is derived from reasoning. When reading a graph, inferences help with interpretation of the data that is being presented. From this information, a **conclusion** and even **predictions** about what the data actually means is possible.

Example: Katherine and Tom were both doing poorly in math class. Their teacher had a conference with each of them in November. The following graph shows their math test scores during the school year.

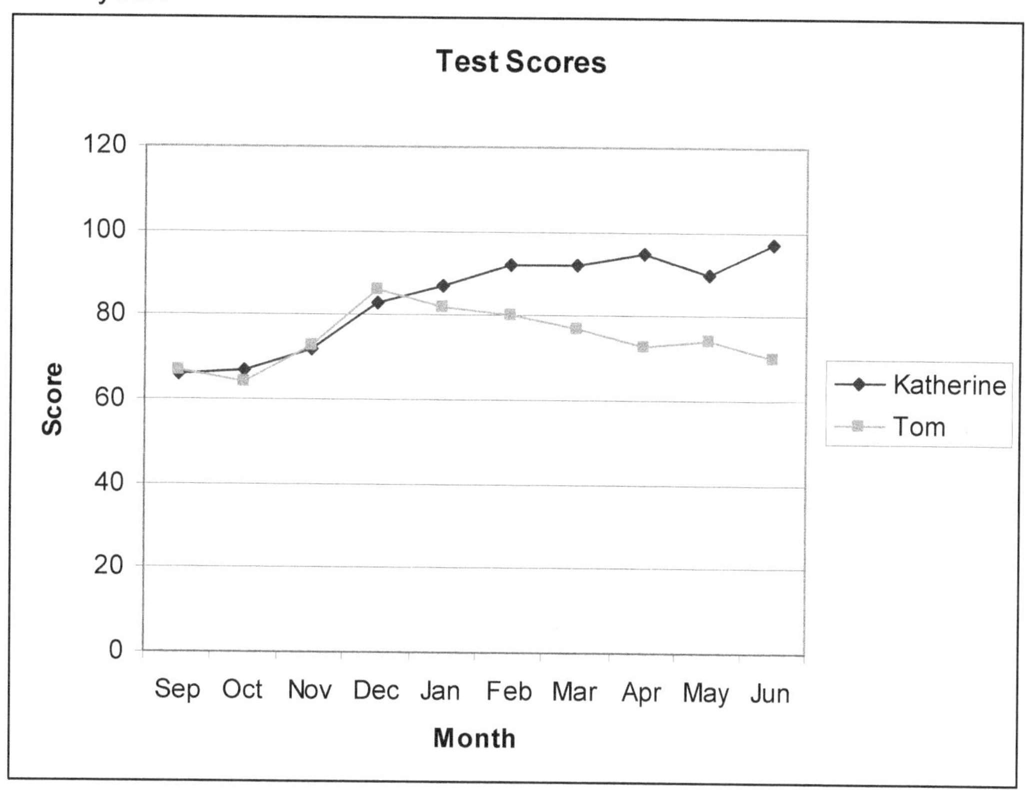

What kind of trend does this graph show?

This graph shows that there is a positive trend in Katherine's test scores and a negative trend in Tom's test scores.

What inferences can you make from this graph?

We can infer that Katherine's test scores rose steadily after November. Tom's test scores spiked in December but then began to fall again and became negatively trended.

What conclusion can you draw based upon this graph?

We can conclude that Katherine took her teacher's meeting seriously and began to study in order to do better on the exams. It seems as though Tom tried harder for a bit, but his test scores eventually slipped back down to the level where he began.

Skill 9.2 Demonstrate the ability to determine the mean, median, and mode of a set of data

The arithmetic **mean** (or average) of a set of numbers is the *sum* of the numbers given, *divided* by the number of items being averaged.

Example: Find the mean. Round to the nearest tenth.
24.6, 57.3, 44.1, 39.8, 64.5
The sum is 230.3 ˜ 5
= 46.06, rounded to 46.1

The **median** of a set is the middle number. To calculate the median, the terms must be arranged in order. If there are an even number of terms, the median is the mean of the two middle terms.

Example: Find the median.

12, 14, 27, 3, 13, 7, 17, 12, 22, 6, 16

Rearrange the terms. 16, 17, 22, 27
3, 6, 7, 12, 12, 13, 14,
Since there are 11 numbers, the middle would be the sixth number or 13.

The **mode** of a set of numbers is the number that occurs with the greatest frequency. A set can have no mode if each term appears exactly one time. Similarly, there can also be more than one mode.

Example: Find the mode.

26, 15, 37, **26,** 35, **26,** 15

15 appears twice, but 26 appears 3 times, therefore the mode is 26.

The **range** is the difference between the highest and lowest value of data items.

Example: Given the ungrouped data below, calculate the mean and range.

15	22	28	25	34	38
18	25	30	33	19	23

Mean ($\overline{X}$) = 25.8333333

Range: $38 - 15 = 23$

Skill 9.3 Demonstrate the ability to represent data in graphic formats

See Skill 9.1.

SAMPLE TEST: MATHEMATICS

1. $\left(\frac{^-4}{9}\right)+\left(\frac{^-7}{10}\right)=$

(Skill 7.1, Rigorous)

A. $\frac{23}{90}$

B. $\frac{^-23}{90}$

C. $\frac{103}{90}$

D. $\frac{^-103}{90}$

2. $(5.6)\times(^-0.11)=$

(Skill 7.1, Average Rigor)

A. $^-0.616$

B. 0.616

C. $^-6.110$

D. 6.110

3. $4\frac{2}{9}$ x $\frac{7}{10}$

(Skill 7.1, Average Rigor)

A. $4\frac{9}{10}$

B. $\frac{266}{90}$

C. $2\frac{43}{45}$

D. $2\frac{6}{20}$

4. 0.74 = (Skill 7.1, Easy)

A. $\frac{74}{100}$

B. 7.4%

C. $\frac{33}{50}$

D. $\frac{74}{10}$

5. $\frac{7}{9}+\frac{1}{3}\div\frac{2}{3}=$
(Skill 7.1, Average Rigor)

A. $\frac{5}{3}$

B. $\frac{3}{2}$

C. 2

D. $\frac{23}{18}$

6. $^{-}9\frac{1}{4}$ □ $^{-}8\frac{2}{3}$
(Skill 7.5, Easy)

A. =

B. <

C. >

D. ≤

7. Round $1\frac{13}{16}$ of an inch to the nearest quarter of an inch. (Skill 7.6, Easy)

A. $1\frac{1}{4}$ inch

B. $1\frac{5}{8}$ inch

C. $1\frac{3}{4}$ inch

D. 2 inches

8. The price of gas was $3.27 per gallon. Your tank holds 15 gallons of fuel. You are using two tanks a week. How much will you save weekly if the price of gas goes down to $2.30 per gallon? (Skill 7.7, Average Rigor)

A. $26.00

B. $29.00

C. $15.00

D. $17.00

9. Given the formula *d* =*rt*, (where *d* = distance, *r* =rate, and *t* =time), calculate the time required for a vehicle to travel 585 miles at a rate of 65 miles per hour. (Skill 7.8, Average Rigor)

A. 8.5 hours

B. 6.5 hours

C. 9.5 hours

D. 9 hours

10. Solve for x.

$$3x - \frac{2}{3} = \frac{5x}{2} + 2$$

(Skill 7.8, Rigorous)

A. $5\frac{1}{3}$

B. $\frac{17}{3}$

C. 2

D. $\frac{16}{2}$

11. Given $f(x) = (x)^3 - 3(x)^2 + 5$, find $x = (-2)$. (Skill 7.8, Rigorous)

A. 15

B. -15

C. 25

D. -25

12. If $4x - (3 - x) = 7(x - 3) + 10$, then (Skill 7.8, Rigorous)

A. $x = 8$

B. $x = -8$

C. $x = 4$

D. $x = -4$

13. 303 is what percent of 600? (Skill 7.9, Average Rigor)

A. 0.505%

B. 5.05%

C. 505%

D. 50.5%

14. An item that sells for $375 is put on sale at $120. What is the percent of decrease? (Skill 7.9, Rigorous)

A. 25%

B. 28%

C. 68%

D. 34%

15. A restaurant employs 465 people. There are 280 waiters and 185 cooks. If 168 waiters and 85 cooks receive pay raises, what percent of the waiters will receive a pay raise? (Skill 7.9, Rigorous)

A. 36.13%

B. 60%

C. 60.22%

D. 40%

16. What measure could be used to report the distance traveled in walking around a track? (Skill 8.2, Average Rigor)

A. degrees

B. square meters

C. kilometers

D. cubic feet

17. What type of triangle is $\triangle ABC$? (Skill 8.3, Rigorous)

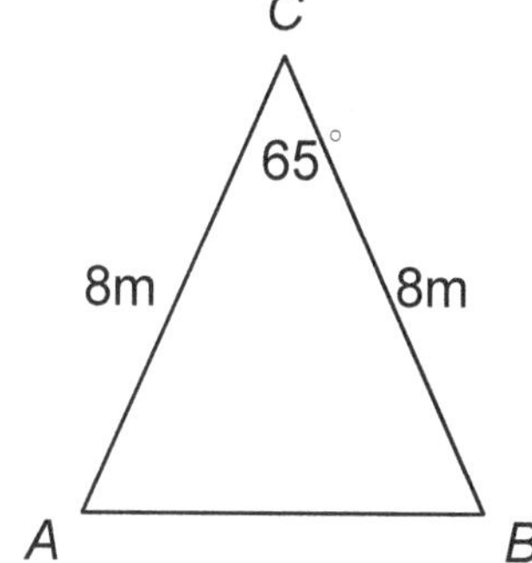

A. right

B. equilateral

C. scalene

D. isosceles

18. The owner of a rectangular piece of land 40 yards in length and 30 yards in width wants to divide it into two parts. She plans to join two opposite corners with a fence as shown in the diagram below. The cost of the fence will be approximately $25 per linear foot. What is the estimated cost for the fence needed by the owner? (Skill 8.4, Rigorous)

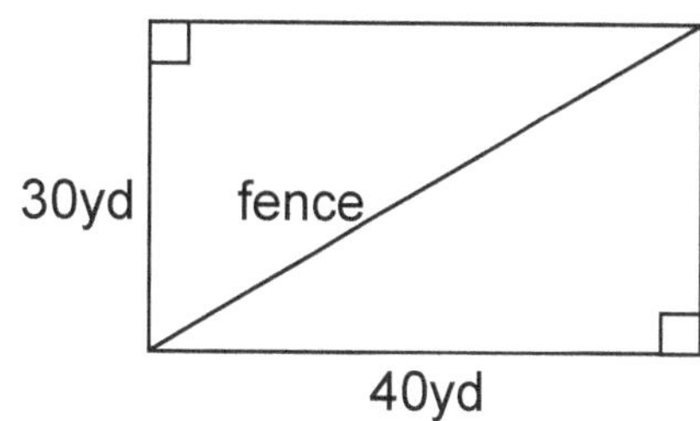

A. $1,250

B. $62,500

C. $5,250

D. $3,750

19. What is the area of a square whose side is 13 feet? (Skill 8.4, Average Rigor)

A. 169 feet

B. 169 square feet

C. 52 feet

D. 52 square feet

20. The trunk of a tree has a 2.1 meter radius. What is its circumference? (Skill 8.4, Average Rigor)

A. 2.1π square meters

B. 4.2π meters

C. 2.1π meters

D. 4.2π square meters

21. Which statement is true about George's budget? (Skill 9.1, Easy)

A. George spends the greatest portion of his income on food.

B. George spends twice as much on utilities as he does on his mortgage.

C. George spends twice as much on utilities as he does on food.

D. George spends the same amount on food and utilities as he does on mortgage.

utilities

mortgage

food

music

22. The following chart shows the yearly average number of international tourists visiting Palm Beach for 1990-1994. How many more international tourists visited Palm Beach in 1994 than in 1991? (Skill 9.1, Average Rigor)

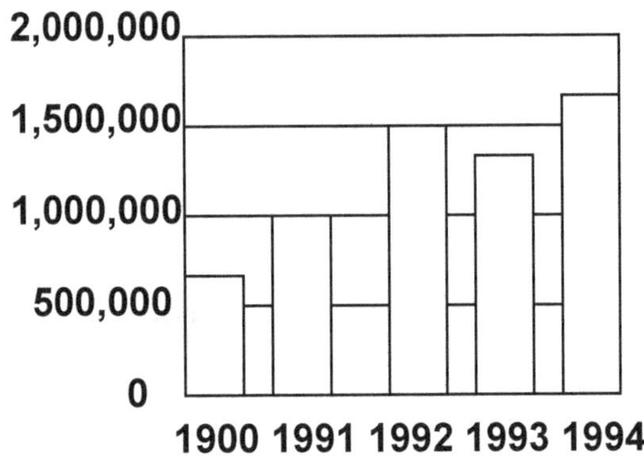

A. 100,000

B. 600,000

C. 1,600,000

D. 8,000,000

23. Consider the graph of the distribution of the length of time it took individuals to complete an employment form. (Skill 9.1, Rigorous)

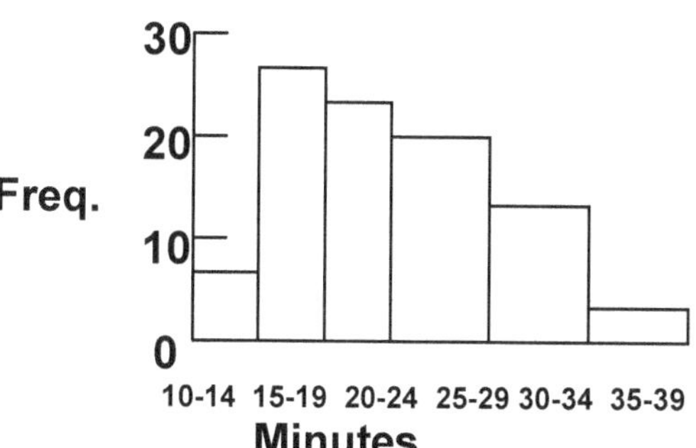

Approximately how many individuals took less than 15 minutes to complete the employment form?

A. 35
B. 28
C. 7
D. 4

24. Mary did comparison shopping on her favorite brand of coffee. Over half of the stores priced the coffee at $1.70. Most of the remaining stores priced the coffee at $1.80, except for a few who charged $1.90. Which of the following statements is true about the distribution of prices? (Skill 9.2, Rigorous)

A. The mean and the mode are the same.
B. The mean is greater than the mode.
C. The mean is less than the mode.
D. The mean is less than the median.

25. What is the mode of the data in the following sample?

9, 10, 11, 9, 10, 11, 9, 13 (Skill 9.2, Easy)

A. 9

B. 9.5

C. 10

D. 11

ANSWER KEY: MATHEMATICS

1. d
2. a
3. c
4. a
5. d
6. b
7. c
8. b
9. d
10. a
11. b
12. c
13. d
14. c
15. b
16. c
17. d
18. d
19. b
20. b
21. c
22. b
23. c
24. b
25. a

RIGOR TABLE: MATHEMATICS

Easy	Average Rigor	Rigorous
Question #s – 4, 6, 7, 21, 25	Question #s – 2,3, 5, 8, 9, 13, 16, 19, 20, 22	Question #s – 1, 10, 11, 12, 14, 15, 17, 18, 23, 24

RATIONALES FOR SAMPLE QUESTIONS: MATHEMATICS

1. $\left(\frac{^-4}{9}\right)+\left(\frac{^-7}{10}\right)=$ **(Skill 7.1, Rigorous)**

A. $\frac{23}{90}$

B. $\frac{^-23}{90}$

C. $\frac{103}{90}$

D. $\frac{^-103}{90}$

The answer is D. Find the least common denominator of $\frac{^-4}{9}$ and $\frac{^-7}{10}$. The LCD is 90, so you get $\frac{^-40}{90}+\frac{^-63}{90}=\frac{^-103}{90}$, which is answer D.

2. $(5.6)\times(^-0.11)=$ **(Skill 7.1, Average Rigor)**

A. $^-0.616$

B. 0.616

C. $^-6.110$

D. 6.110

The answer is A. Simple multiplication. The answer will be negative because a positive times a negative is a negative number. $5.6\times{}^-0.11={}^-0.616$, which is answer A.

3. $4\frac{2}{9} \times \frac{7}{10}$ **(Skill 7.1, Average Rigor)**

A. $4\frac{9}{10}$

B. $\frac{266}{90}$

C. $2\frac{43}{45}$

D. $2\frac{6}{20}$

The answer is C. Convert any mixed number to an improper fraction: $\frac{38}{9} x \frac{7}{10}$. Since no common factors of numerators or denominators exist, multiply the numerators and the denominators by each other = $\frac{266}{90}$. Convert back to a mixed number and reduce $2\frac{86}{90} = 2\frac{43}{45}$.

4. 0.74 = (Skill 7.1, Easy)

A. $\frac{74}{100}$

B. 7.4%

C. $\frac{33}{50}$

D. $\frac{74}{10}$

The answer is A. 0.74→the 4 is in the hundredths place, so the answer is $\frac{74}{100}$, which is A.

5. $\frac{7}{9}+\frac{1}{3}\div\frac{2}{3}=$ **(Skill 7.1, Average Rigor)**

A. $\frac{5}{3}$

B. $\frac{3}{2}$

C. 2

D. $\frac{23}{18}$

The answer is D. First, do the division.

$\frac{1}{3}\div\frac{2}{3}=\frac{1}{3}\times\frac{3}{2}=\frac{1}{2}$

Add.

$\frac{7}{9}+\frac{1}{2}=\frac{14}{18}+\frac{9}{18}=\frac{23}{18}$, which is answer D.

6. $^{-}9\frac{1}{4}$ □ $^{-}8\frac{2}{3}$ **(Skill 7.5, Easy)**

A. =

B. <

C. >

D. ≤

The answer is B. The larger the absolute value of a negative number, the smaller the negative number is. The absolute value of $-9\frac{1}{4}$ is $9\frac{1}{4}$ which is larger than the absolute value of $-8\frac{2}{3}$ is $8\frac{2}{3}$. Therefore, the sign should be $-9\frac{1}{4}<-8\frac{2}{3}$, which is answer B.

7. Round $1\frac{13}{16}$ of an inch to the nearest quarter of an inch. (Skill 7.6, Easy)

A. $1\frac{1}{4}$ inch

B. $1\frac{5}{8}$ inch

C. $1\frac{3}{4}$ inch

D. 2 inches

The answer is C. $1\frac{13}{16}$ inches is approximately $1\frac{12}{16}$, which is also $1\frac{3}{4}$, which is the nearest $\frac{1}{4}$ of an inch, so the answer is C.

8. The price of gas was $3.27 per gallon. Your tank holds 15 gallons of fuel. You are using two tanks a week. How much will you save weekly if the price of gas goes down to $2.30 per gallon? (Skill 7.7, Average Rigor)

A. $26.00

B. $29.00

C. $15.00

D. $17.00

The answer is B. 15 gallons x 2 tanks = 30 gallons a week = 30 gallons x $3.27 = $98.10
30 gallons x $2.30 = $69.00
$98.10 - $69.00 = $29.10 is approximately $29.00. The answer is B.

9. Given the formula *d* =*rt*, (where *d* = distance, *r* =rate, and *t* =time), calculate the time required for a vehicle to travel 585 miles at a rate of 65 miles per hour. (Skill 7.8, Average Rigor)

A. 8.5 hours

B. 6.5 hours

C. 9.5 hours

D. 9 hours

The answer is D. We are given d = 585 miles and r = 65 miles per hour and $d=rt$. Solve for t. $585 = 65t \rightarrow t = 9$ hours, which is answer D.

10. Solve for x.

$$3x - \frac{2}{3} = \frac{5x}{2} + 2$$

(Skill 7.8, Rigorous)

A. $5\frac{1}{3}$

B. $\frac{17}{3}$

C. 2

D. $\frac{16}{2}$

The answer is A. $3x(6) - \frac{2}{3}(6) = \frac{5x}{2}(6) + 2(6)$ 6 is the lowest common denominator of 2 and 3

$$18x - 4 = 15x + 12$$
$$18x = 15x + 16$$
$$3x = 16$$
$$x = \frac{16}{3} = 5\frac{1}{3}$$

, which is answer A.

11. Given $f(x) = (x)^3 - 3(x)^2 + 5$,find x = (-2). (Skill 7.8, Rigorous)

A. 15

B. -15

C. 25

D. -25

The answer is B.

Substitute x = -2.

$$f(-2) = (^-2)^3 - 3 \times (^-2)^2 + 5$$
$$f(-2) = {}^-8 - 3(4) + 5$$
$$f(-2) = {}^-8 - 12 + 5$$
$$f(-2) = {}^-15$$

12. If $4x - (3 - x) = 7(x - 3) + 10$, then (Skill 7.8, Rigorous)

A. $x = 8$

B. $x = -8$

C. $x = 4$

D. $x = -4$

The answer is C. Solve for x.

$$4x - (3 - x) = 7(x - 3) + 10$$
$$4x - 3 + x = 7x - 21 + 10$$
$$5x - 3 = 7x - 11$$
$$5x = 7x - 11 + 3$$
$$5x - 7x = {}^-8$$
$$^-2x = {}^-8$$
$$x = 4$$

13. 303 is what percent of 600? (Skill 7.9, Average Rigor)

A. 0.505%

B. 5.05%

C. 505%

D. 50.5%

The answer is D. Use *x* for the percent. $600x = 303.$
$\frac{600x}{600} = \frac{303}{600} \rightarrow x = 0.505 = 50.5\%$, which is answer D.

14. An item that sells for $375 is put on sale at $120. What is the percent of decrease? (Skill 7.9, Rigorous)

A. 25%

B. 28%

C. 68%

D. 34%

The answer is C. Use (1 – *x*) as the discount. $375x = 120$.
$375(1-x) = 120 \rightarrow 375 - 375x = 120 \rightarrow 375x = 255 \rightarrow x = 0.68$ = 68%, which is answer C.

15. A restaurant employs 465 people. There are 280 waiters and 185 cooks. If 168 waiters and 85 cooks receive pay raises, what percent of the waiters will receive a pay raise? (Skill 7.9, Rigorous)

A. 36.13%

B. 60%

C. 60.22%

D. 40%

The answer is B. The total number of waiters is 280 and only 168 of them get a pay raise. Divide the number getting a raise by the total number of waiters to get the percent. $\frac{168}{280} = 0.6 = 60\%$, which is answer B.

16. What measure could be used to report the distance traveled in walking around a track? (Skill 8.2, Average Rigor)

A. degrees

B. square meters

C. kilometers

D. cubic feet

The answer is C. Degrees measures angles, square meters measures area, cubic feet measure volume, and kilometers measures length. Kilometers is the only reasonable answer, which is C.

17. What type of triangle is $\triangle ABC$? (Skill 8.3, Rigorous)

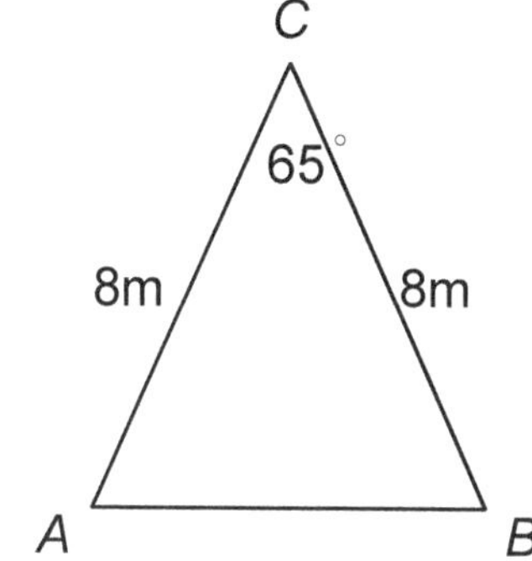

A. right

B. equilateral

C. scalene

D. isosceles

The answer is D. Two of the sides are the same length, so we know the triangle is either equilateral or isosceles. $\measuredangle CAB$ and $\measuredangle CBA$ are equal, because their sides are. Therefore, $180^\circ = 65^\circ - 2x = \frac{115^\circ}{2} = 57.5^\circ$. Because all three angles are not equal, the triangle is isosceles, so the answer is D.

18. The owner of a rectangular piece of land 40 yards in length and 30 yards in width wants to divide it into two parts. She plans to join two opposite corners with a fence as shown in the diagram below. The cost of the fence will be approximately $25 per linear foot. What is the estimated cost for the fence needed by the owner? (Skill 8.4, Rigorous)

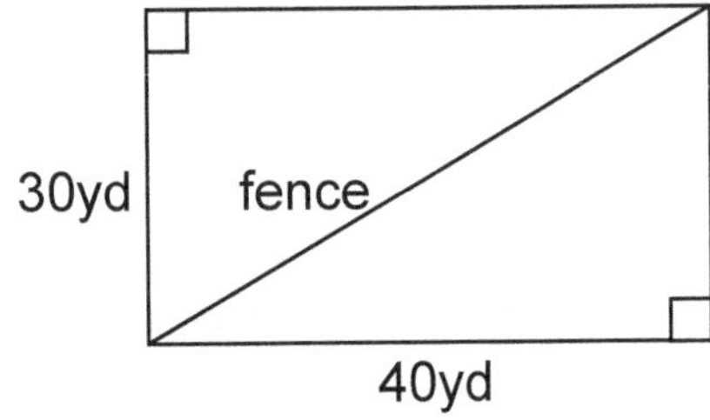

A. $1,250

B. $62,500

C. $5,250

D. $3,750

The answer is D. Find the length of the diagonal by using the Pythagorean theorem. Let *x* be the length of the diagonal.

$$30^2 + 40^2 = x^2 \rightarrow 900 + 1600 = x^2$$
$$2500 = x^2 \rightarrow \sqrt{2500} = \sqrt{x^2}$$
$$x = 50 \text{ yards}$$

Convert to feet. $\frac{50 \text{ yards}}{x \text{ feet}} = \frac{1 \text{ yard}}{3 \text{ feet}} \rightarrow 1500 \text{ feet}$

It cost $25.00 per linear foot, so the cost is (1500 ft)($25) = $3750, which is answer D.

19. What is the area of a square whose side is 13 feet? (Skill 8.4, Average Rigor)

A. 169 feet

B. 169 square feet

C. 52 feet

D. 52 square feet

The answer is B.
Area = length times width (*lw*).
Length = 13 feet
Width = 13 feet (square, so length and width are the same).
Area = $13 \times 13 = 169$ square feet.
Area is measured in square feet.

20. The trunk of a tree has a 2.1 meter radius. What is its circumference? (Skill 8.4, Average Rigor)

A. 2.1π square meters

B. 4.2π meters

C. $2.1\ \pi$ meters

D. 4.2π square meters

The answer is B. Circumference is $2\pi r$, where r is the radius. The circumference is $2\pi 2.1 = 4.2\pi$ meters (not square meters because not measuring area), which is answer B.

21. Which statement is true about George's budget? (Skill 9.1, Easy)

A. George spends the greatest portion of his income on food.

B. George spends twice as much on utilities as he does on his mortgage.

C. George spends twice as much on utilities as he does on food.

D. George spends the same amount on food and utilities as he does on mortgage.

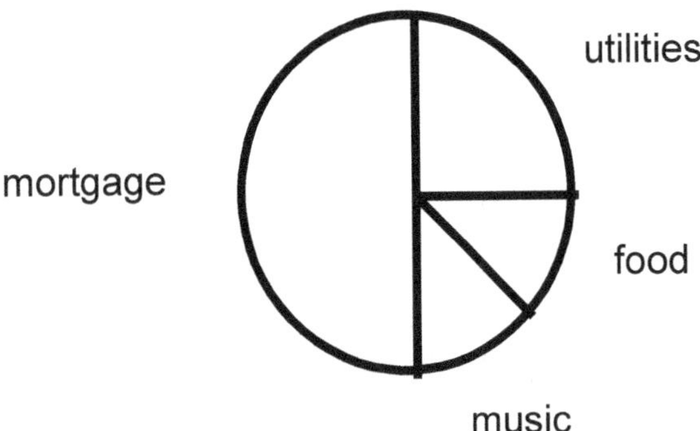

The answer is C. George spends twice as much on utilities as he does on food. George spends twice as much on utilities as on food.

22. The following chart shows the yearly average number of international tourists visiting Palm Beach for 1990-1994. How many more international tourists visited Palm Beach in 1994 than in 1991? (Skill 9.1, Average Rigor)

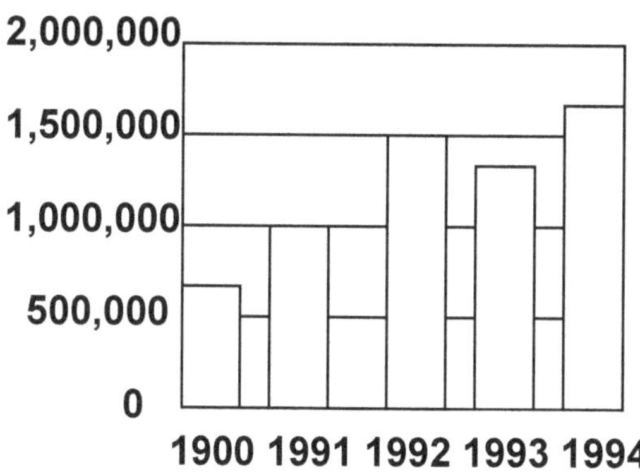

A. 100,000

B. 600,000

C. 1,600,000

D. 8,000,000

The answer is B. The number of tourists in 1991 was 1,000,000 and the number in 1994 was 1,600,000. Subtract to get a difference of 600,000, which is answer B.

23. Consider the graph of the distribution of the length of time it took individuals to complete an employment form. (Skill 9.1, Rigorous)

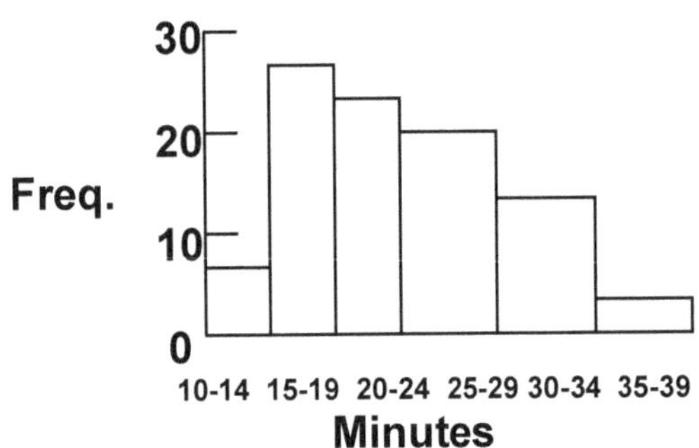

Approximately how many individuals took less than 15 minutes to complete the employment form?

A. 35
B. 28
C. 7
D. 4

The answer is C. According to the chart, the number of people who took under 15 minutes is 7, which is answer C.

24. Mary did comparison shopping on her favorite brand of coffee. Over half of the stores priced the coffee at $1.70. Most of the remaining stores priced the coffee at $1.80, except for a few who charged $1.90. Which of the following statements is true about the distribution of prices? (Skill 9.2, Rigorous)

A. The mean and the mode are the same.
B. The mean is greater than the mode.
C. The mean is less than the mode.
D. The mean is less than the median.

The answer is B. Over half the stores priced the coffee at $1.70, so this means that this is the mode. The mean would be slightly over $1.70 because other stores priced the coffee at over $1.70.

25. What is the mode of the data in the following sample?

9, 10, 11, 9, 10, 11, 9, 13 (Skill 9.2, Easy)

A. 9

B. 9.5

C. 10

D. 11

The answer is A. The mode is the number that appears most frequently. 9 appears 3 times, which is more than the other numbers. Therefore the answer is A.

COMPETENCY 10.0 UNDERSTAND THE APPLICATION OF READING SKILLS TO CLASSROOM INSTRUCTION

Skill 10.1 Recognize elements of phonics (e.g., long and short vowels) and how words are formed (e.g., syllables, root words, prefixes, suffixes)

For children, the ability to identify vowel-sound combinations and syllabic words is contingent on familiarity of sounds that when combined can produce identifiable words. There are vowel sound essentials that create visual opportunities for children learning the phonics of vowel letter combinations. Children who are able to memorize all of the vowel sounds will learn how to spell and read faster, according to researchers.

The vowel sound essentials include the following vowel letter combinations:

- Short vowels: a, e, i, o, and u
- Long vowels: a, e, i, o, and u
- Diagraphs (2 letters that produce 1 sound): ai, ee, ie, oa, ay, au, and aw
- Diphthongs (2 letters with 2 sounds): ou, oo-long/short, ew, ow-long/short, oi
- R vowels: ar, er, ir, or, ur

When children are encouraged to identify and memorize the basic vowel sound essentials, they are able to synthesize their learning into the decoding of new words and text. In most school communities, children are taught the memorization of basic consonants' sounds but not the memorization of vowel sound essentials.

The application of vowel sounds to syllabic words creates an additional avenue of reading and word meaning support for children increasing reading ability and word usage. Children who have an understanding and memorization of the vowel sound essentials are able to increase their decoding strategy of new words by a higher percentage than children who base comprehension on predictable text of known words and usage.

In syllabic understanding, children are being asked to understand the organization of a sequence of speech sounds that formalize words. Syllables are word building blocks that provide pronunciation patterns and rhythm to language. Monosyllable words such as "cat" or "hat" consist of speech patterns that use consonants and vowels to form a singular sound. As words become more complex in syllabic construct, they can consist of two syllables, disyllable ("read-er") up to more than four syllables, polysyllable (i.e. "com-mun-i-ca-tion").

The phonetics of syllabic words includes a core nucleus of vowel sounds that can be viewed in common words as a "consonant-vowel-consonant" sequence of letters and sounds. Longer syllabic words such as "imagination" have stress and tone on each part of the syllabic segments that includes a phonetic emphasis on the core nucleus of the word. Children learning to understand the contextual meaning of words must understand the vowel and syllabic construction to word formation and usage.

Syllabification as a Word Identification Strategy

Another way to help students identify words is to help them understand syllabification. Here is only one of many games that you can use.

Clap Hands, Count those Syllables as They Come!! (Taberski, 2000)

The objective of this activity is for children to understand that every syllable in a polysyllabic word can be studied for its spelling patterns in the same way that monosyllabic words are studied for their spelling patterns.

The easiest way for the K-3 teacher to introduce this activity to the children is to share a familiar poem from the poetry chart (or to write out a familiar poem on a large experiential chart).

First the teacher reads the poem with the children. As they are reading it aloud, the children clap the beats of the poem and the teacher uses a colored marker to place a tic (/) above each syllable.

Next, the teacher takes letter cards and selects one of the polysyllabic words from the poem which the children have already "clapped" out.

The children use letter cards to spell that word on the sentence strip holder or it can be placed on a felt board or up against a window on display. Together the children and teacher divide the letters into syllables and place blank letter cards between the syllables. The children identify spelling patterns they know.

Finally, and as part of continued small group syllabification study, the children identify other polysyllabic words they clapped out from the poem. They make up the letter combinations of these words. Then they separate them into syllables with blank letter cards between the syllables.

Children who require special support in syllabification can be encouraged to use many letter cards to create a large butcher paper syllabic (in letter cards with spaces) representation of the poem or at least a few lines of the poem. They can be told that this is for use as a teaching tool for others. In this way, they authenticate their study of syllabification with a real product that can actually be referenced by peers.

Decoding Strategies
The following activity is presented in detail so it can actually be implemented with children in an intermediate classroom. The detail will help you prepare for a potential constructed response question on a certification examination.

The CVC phonics card game developed by Jackie Montierth, a computer teacher in South San Diego for use with 5th and 6th grade students, is a good one to adapt to the needs of any group with appropriate modifications for age, grade level, and language needs.

The children use the vehicle of the card game to practice and enhance their use of consonants and vowels. Their fluency in this will increase their ability to decode words. Potential uses beyond whole classroom instruction include use as part of the small group word work component of the reading workshop and as part of cooperative team learning. This particular strategy also is particularly helpful for grade four and beyond English language learners who are in a regular English language classroom setting.

The card game works well because the practice of the content is implicit for transfer as the children continue to improve their reading skills. In addition, the card game format allows "instructional punctuation" using a student-centered high interest exploration.

Card Design: To create a deck, use the computer, 5"x 8" index cards, or actual card deck-sized oak tag cards. For repeated use and durability, be sure to laminate the cards.

The deck should consist of the following:

- 44 consonant cards (including the blends)
- 15 vowel cards (including 3 of each vowel)
- 5 wild cards (which can be used as any vowel)
- 6 final e cards

The design of this project can also focus on particular CVC words that are part of a particular book, topic, or genre format. In advance of playing the game, children can also be directed to review the words on the word wall or other words on a word map.

Procedure: Introduce the game first as part of a mini lesson. Read the rules and have a pair of children demonstrate. Have the children divide into pairs or small groups of no more than four per group. Each group needs one deck of CVC cards.

Have each group choose a dealer. The dealer shuffles the cards and deals five cards to each player. The remaining cards are placed face down for drawing during the play. One card is turned over to form the discard pile. Players may not show their cards to the other players. The first player to the left of the dealer looks at the cards and, if possible, puts down three cards which make a consonant-vowel-consonant word. For more points, four cards forming a consonant-vowel-consonant word can be placed down. The player must then say the word and draw the number of cards to replace the cards that were laid down. If the player is unable to form a word, the player draws a card either from the draw or discard pile. The player then discards one card. All players must have five cards at all times. Play moves to the left.

The game continues until one or more of the following happens:

1. There are no more cards in the draw pile.
2. All players run out of cards.
3. All players cannot form a word.

The winner is the player who has laid down the most cards during the game. Players may only lay down words at the beginning of their turn. Proper names may not be counted as words.

Variations: The game can be played with teams in a small group of four or fewer competing against one another (which is excellent for special needs or resource room students). It can also be done as a whole class activity where all the students are divided into cooperative teams or small groups who compete against one another. This second approach will work well with a heterogeneous classroom that includes special needs and/or ELL children.

Teachers of ELL learners can do this game in the native language first and then transition it into English, facilitating native language reading skills and second language acquisition. They can develop their own appropriate decks to meet the vocabulary needs of their children and to complement the curricula.

Using Phonics to Decode Words in Connected Text

Identifying New Words: Some strategies to share with children during conferences or as part of shared reading include the following prompts:

- Look at the beginning letter/s. What sound do you hear?
- Stop to think about the text or story. What word with this beginning letter would make sense here?
- Look at the book's illustrations. Do they provide you with help in figuring out the new word?
- Think of what word would make sense, sound right, and match the letters that you see. Start the sentence over, making your mouth ready to say that word.

- Skip the word, read to the end of the sentence, and then come back to the word. How does what you've read help you with the word?
- Listen to whether what you are reading makes sense and matches the letters (asking the child to self-monitor). If it doesn't make sense, see if you can correct it on your own.
- Look for spelling patterns you know from the spelling pattern wall.
- Look for smaller words you might know within the larger word.
- Read on a little, and then return to the part that confused you.

Techniques for Identifying Compound Words

The teaching of compound words should use structural analysis techniques such as the game described above. Here are some other strategies for helping students to identify and read compound words.

- Use songs and actions to help children understand the concept that compound words are two smaller words joined together to make one bigger word.
- Use games like Concentration, Memory and Go Fish for students to practice reading compound words.
- Use word sorts to have students distinguish between compound words and nonexamples of compound words.

Identification of Homographs

Homographs are words that are spelled the same but have different meanings. A subgroup within this area includes words that are spelled the same, have different meanings, and are pronounced differently. Some examples of homographs include "lie," "tear," "bow," "fair," "bass."

Teaching homographs can be interesting and fun for the students. Incorporate them into passages where the students can use the context clues to decipher the different meanings of the homographs. Games are also a good strategy for using to help students understand multiple meaning words. Jokes and riddles are usually based on homographs, and students love to make collections or books of these.

Structural Analysis

Structural analysis of words as defined by J. David Cooper (2004) involves the study of significant word parts. This analysis can help the child with pronunciation and constructing meaning.

This aspect of vocabulary development is to help children look for structural elements within words which they can use independently to help them determine meaning.

Some teachers choose to directly teach structural analysis. In particular, those who teach by following the phonics-centered approach for reading do this. Other teachers, who follow the balanced literacy approach, introduce the structural components as part of mini lessons that are focused on the students' reading and writing.

The term list below is generally recognized as the key structural analysis components.

Root Word is a word from which another word is developed. The second word can be said to have its "root" in the first, such as *vis, to see,* in visor or vision. This structural component can be illustrated by a tree with roots to display the meaning for children. Children may also want to literally construct root words using cardboard trees to create word family models.

Prefixes are beginning units of meaning which can be added (the vocabulary word for this type of structural adding is "affixed") to a base word or root word. They can not stand alone. They are also sometimes known as "bound morphemes" meaning that they can not stand alone as a base word. Examples are *re-, un-*, and *mis-*.

Suffixes are ending units of meaning which can be "affixed" or added on to the ends of root or base words. Suffixes transform the original meanings of base and root words. Like prefixes, they are also known as "bound morphemes," because they can not stand alone as words. Examples are *-less, -ful*, and *-tion*.

Compound Words occur when two or more base words are connected to form a new word. The meaning of the new word is in some way connected with that of the base word. Examples are *firefighter, newspaper*, and *pigtail*.

Inflectional Endings are types of suffixes that impart a new meaning to the base or root word. These endings in particular change the gender, number, tense, or form of the base or root words. Just like other suffixes, these are also termed "bound morphemes." Examples are *–s* or *-ed*.

Learn more about
Word Analysis
http://www.orangeusd.k12.ca.us/yorba/word_analysis.htm

Base Words are stand-alone linguistic units which cannot be deconstructed or broken down into smaller words. For example, in the word re-tell, the base word is *tell*.

Contractions are shortened forms of two words in which a letter or letters have been deleted. These deleted letters have been replaced by an apostrophe. Examples are *can't, didn't, I've* and *wouldn't*.

Phoneme: A phoneme is the smallest unit of sound in the English language. In print phonemes are represented by the letter and a slash. So, /b/ represents the sound the letter b would make.

Morpheme: A morpheme is the smallest unit of grammar in the English language. In other words, it is the smallest unit of meaning, not just sounds.

Consonant Digraph: A consonant digraph is two consonants of the English language placed together in a word to make a unique sound neither makes when alone. Examples: ch, th, sh, and wh.

Consonant Blend: A consonant blend occurs when two consonants are put together but each retains its individual sound. The two sounds go together in a seamless manner to produce a blended sound. Examples: st, br, cl.

Schwa sound: A schwa sound is a neutral vowel sound. It typically occurs in the unaccented syllable of a word. An example would be the sound of the /a/ at the end of the word sofa. It is represented in print by an upside down e /ə/.

Skill 10.2 Demonstrate knowledge of techniques for decoding text using context clues

Students will inevitably come across words they are unable to read. When this happens, they will need a variety of strategies to draw upon not only to figure out the unknown word but also to be able to gather meaning from the word and text.

Students typically begin with decoding, or the application of phonics skills, when they come across an unknown word. If they are unable to correctly decode the word, they may use some other strategies including structural analysis and context clues.

To decode means to change communication signals into messages. Reading comprehension requires that the reader learn the code within which a message is written and be able to decode it to get the message.

Although effective reading comprehension requires identifying words automatically (Adams, 1990, Perfetti, 1985), children do not have to be able to identify every single word or know the exact meaning of the every word in a text to understand it. Indeed, Nagy (1988) says that, children can read a work with a high level of comprehension even if they do not fully know as many as 15 percent of the words within a given text.

Children develop the ability to decode and recognize words automatically. They then can extend their ability to decode to multi-syllabic words.

J. David Cooper (2004) and other advocates of the Balanced Literacy Approach, feel that children become literate, effective communicators and able to comprehend, by learning phonics and other aspects of word identification through the use of engaging reading texts. Engaging text, as defined by the balanced literacy group, are those texts which contain highly predictable elements of rhyme, sound patterns, and plot. Researchers, such as Chall (1983) and Flesch (1981), support a phonics-centered foundation before the use of engaging reading texts. This is at the crux of the phonics versus whole language/ balanced literacy/ integrated language arts, teaching of reading controversy.

As a teacher, you should be familiar with both sides of this controversy as well as the work of theorists who attempt to reconcile these two perspectives, such as Kenneth Goodman (1994). There are powerful arguments on both sides of this controversy, and each approach works wonderfully with some students and does not succeed with others.

As a working teacher you can choose from the strategies and approaches which work best for the children concerned, depending on the perspective of your school administration and the needs of the particular children you serve.

Contextual Redefinition

This strategy encourages children to use the context more effectively by presenting them with sufficient context *before* they begin reading. It models for the children the use of contextual clues to make informed guesses about word meanings.

To apply this strategy, you should first select unfamiliar words for teaching. No more than two or three words should be selected for direct teaching. You should then write a sentence in which sufficient clues are supplied for the child to figure out the meaning successfully. Among the types of context clues you can use are compare/contrast, synonyms, and direct definition.

Then present the words only on the experiential chart or as letter cards. Have the children pronounce the words. As they pronounce them, challenge them to come up with a definition for each word. After more than one definition is offered, encourage the children to decide as a whole group what the definition is. Write down their agreed upon definition with no comment as to its accurate meaning.

Then share with the children the contexts (sentences that you wrote with the words and explicit context clues). Ask that the children to read the sentences aloud. Then have them come up with a definition for each word. Do not comment as they present their definitions. Ask that they justify their definitions by making specific references to the context clues in the sentences. As the discussion continues, direct the children's attention to their previously agreed-upon definition of the word. Facilitate their discussing the differences between their guesses about the word when they saw only the word itself and their guesses about the word when they read it in context. Finally have the children check their use of context skills to correctly define the word by using a dictionary.

A good strategy to use in working with individual children is to have them explain how they finally correctly identified a word that was troubling them. If prompted and habituated through one-on-one teacher/tutoring conversations, they can be quite clear about what they did to "get" the word.

If the children are already writing their own stories, the teacher might say to them: "You know when you write your own stories you would never write any story which did not make sense. You wouldn't, and probably this writer didn't either. If you read something that does make sense, but doesn't match the letters, then it's probably not what the author wrote. This is the author's story, not yours right now, so go back to the word and see if you can find out the author's story. Later on, you might write your own story."

Use of Semantic and Syntactic Cues to Help Decode Words

Semantic Cues

Students will need use their base knowledge of word meanings—semantics—to help them decipher unknown words or text as well as to clarify reading when it does not seem to make sense. Some prompts the teacher can use which will alert the children to semantic cues include:

- Does that sentence make sense?
- Which word in that sentence does not seem to fit?
- Why doesn't it fit?
- What word might make sense in that sentence?

Syntactic Cues

The first strategy good readers use from their own knowledge base to help determine misreading is syntactic cues. Syntactic cues use the order of words and the student's knowledge of the oral English language to determine if what was read could be accurate. Some prompts the teacher can use to encourage and develop syntactic cues in reading include:

- You read (child's incorrect attempt). Does that sound right?
- You read (child's incorrect attempt). When we talk, do we talk that way?

- How would we say it?
- Recheck that sentence. Does it sound right the way you read it?

Contextual reading is something we all do from a very young age to adult years. Sometimes regardless the ability to decode or apply structural analysis, there are words we are still unable to read. In this case, the reader can use other words in the sentence or paragraph to help decide the unknown word.

Good readers use the syntax, or the manner in which the sentence is put together, to help determine meaning from context. They also find ways to put the sentence or passage in their own words or look for contrasting ideas. All of these strategies help the reader to draw meaning from what is being read. This frame of reference helps to provide more details for the reader. Contrast is also a method readers may use to build context or determine meaning.

Skill 10.3 Demonstrate knowledge of prereading strategies for students (e.g., skimming, making predictions)

Throughout their lives students will be reading for a variety of purposes and with a multitude of different texts. The purpose behind reading often drives the type of reading completed by the student. The type of text can also drive the type of reading strategies the students use to successfully navigate the information.

Just jumping into a reading assignment may be tempting. Most students just want to get the assignment done and are unwilling to add any steps. Persuading them that they will save time in the end if they will take the time to do some preliminary preparation for reading a piece will be worth the classroom time.

Check out different
Reading Strategies
http://www.greece.k12.ny.us/instruction/ela/6-12/Reading/Reading%20Strategies/reading%20strategies%20index.htm

So what can be done ahead of time? Looking at the date of publication is useful. Knowing that a story, for example, was published in 1930 or in 2005 tells a lot about the setting and characters. Knowing what was going on in the world at that time would also be useful, and an encyclopedia can provide a quick overview. Also, knowing something about the author is useful. Where did the author grow up? What is known about the author's background? Most well-known authors will have at least a short biography in an appropriate encyclopedia.

A quick overview of the story before beginning to read can also be useful. Are there chapters with headings? If not, a quick survey of the sections, either chapters or paragraphs, will yield clues that will guide the reading and improve comprehension.

Skimming

If the reading assignment is an essay, a quick skimming for paragraph topic sentences and a look at the conclusion will provide useful information before beginning the actual reading. Students should be warned not to make premature judgments based on any of these pre-reading activities and advised to let the story or essay speak for itself.

When reading for pleasure, students tend to read less carefully and they may even skim some portions of the text. As the book is simply for pleasure, this is perfectly acceptable and should be allowed. In fact, skimming skills can be introduced and used for other types of readings. Students who are looking for vocabulary words or definitions may skim a great deal of information at a more rapid pace before finding the appropriate part of the passage. This is also a good strategy when used to find any specific pieces of information.

In addition to skimming, scanning is another technique students can use to look through a large amount of text for specific details and/or information. This can be particularly helpful in searching through different books to determine if any of the information is pertinent to meet the needs of the student.

Making Predictions

One theory or approach to the teaching of reading that gained currency in the late sixties and the early seventies was the importance of asking inferential and critical thinking questions of the reader which would challenge and engage the children in the text. This approach to reading went beyond the literal level of what was stated in the text to an inferential level of using text clues to make predictions and to a critical level of involving the child in evaluating the text. While asking engaging and thought-provoking questions is still viewed as part of the teaching of reading, it is only viewed currently as a component of the teaching of reading.

Rereading Information

Teachers need to teach students when it is necessary to reread information. Typically, students understand that it is important to reread when something is not understood clearly. However, there are other times when rereading may be important. In content-heavy texts, rereading can not only provide further clarification, but it can also provide additional details the reader may have missed the first time. It is easy to miss information when so much is packed into small passages. Thus, rereading can be an important factor in learning and making sure they have taken in all of the details.

In-depth reading can be a fatiguing task and cannot be completed on all books students will encounter. Reading with the specific eye for details, students need to understand this process and that it is called for mostly in nonfiction texts which are laden with information. When reading in depth, students are trying to intake as much information as possible. It requires concentration and a concerted effort.

Skill 10.4 Demonstrate knowledge of methods for determining how well students are comprehending what they read

Students need to be aware of their comprehension, or lack of it, in particular texts. So, it is important to teach students what to do when suddenly text stops making sense. For example, students can go back and re-read the description of a character. Or, they can go back to the table of contents or the first paragraph of a chapter to see where they are headed

Learn more about
Monitoring Comprehension
http://www.indiana.edu/~l517/monitoring.html

Comprehension simply means that the reader can ascribe meaning to text. Even though students may be good with phonics and even know what many words on a page mean, some of them are not strong with comprehension because they do not know the strategies that would help them to comprehend. For example, students should know that stories often have structures (beginning, middle, and end). They should also know that when they are reading something and it does not make sense, they will need to employ "fix-up" strategies where they go back into the text they just read and look for clues. Teachers can use many strategies to teach comprehension, including questioning, asking students to paraphrase or summarize, using graphic organizers, and focusing on mental images.

The point of comprehension instruction is not necessarily to focus just on the text(s) students are using at the very moment of instruction, but rather to help them learn the strategies that they can use independently with any other text. Some of the most common methods of teaching instruction are as follows:

- Question answering: While this tends to be over-used in many classrooms, it is still a valid method of teaching students to comprehend. As the name implies, students answer questions regarding a text, either out loud, in small groups, or individually on paper. The best questions are those that cause students to have to think about the text (rather than just find an answer within the text).

- Question generating: This is the opposite of question answering, although students can then be asked to answer their own questions or the questions of peer students. In general, we want students to constantly question texts as they read. This is important because it causes students to become more critical readers. To teach students to generate questions helps them to learn the types of questions they can ask, and it gets them thinking about how best to be critical of texts.

- Graphic organizers: Graphic organizers are graphical representations of content within a text. For example, Venn diagrams can be used to highlight the difference between two characters in a novel or two similar political concepts in a social studies textbook. Or, a teacher can use flow-charts with students to talk about the steps in a process (for example, the steps of setting up a science experiment or the chronological events of a story). Semantic organizers are similar in that they graphically display information. The difference, usually, is that semantic organizers focus on words or concepts. For example, a word web can help students make sense of a word by mapping from the central word all the similar and related concepts to that word.

- Text structure: Often in non-fiction, particularly in textbooks, and sometimes in fiction, text structures will give important clues to readers about what to look for. Often, students do not know how to make sense of all the types of headings in a textbook and do not realize that, for example, the side-bar story about a character in history is not the main text on a particular page in the history textbook. Teaching students how to interpret text structures gives them tools in which to tackle other similar texts.

- Monitoring comprehension: Students need to be aware of their comprehension, or lack of it, in particular texts. So, you should teach students what to do when suddenly text stops making sense. For example, students can go back and re-read the description of a character. Or, they can go back to the table of contents or the first paragraph of a chapter to see where they are headed.

- Textual marking: This is where students interact with the text as they read. For example, armed with post-it notes, students can insert questions or comments regarding specific sentences or paragraphs within the text. This helps students focus on the importance of the small things, particularly when they are reading larger works (such as novels in high school). It also gives students a reference point on which to go back into the text when they need to review something.

Many people mistakenly believe that the terms "research-based" or "research-validated" or "evidence-based" relate mainly to specific programs, such as early reading textbook programs. While research does validate that some of these programs are effective, much research has been conducted regarding the effectiveness of particular instructional strategies. In reading, many of these strategies have been documented in the report from the National Reading Panel (2000).

However, just because a strategy has not been validated as effective by research does not necessarily mean that it is not effective with certain students in certain situations. The number of strategies out there far outweighs researchers' ability to test their effectiveness. Some of the strategies listed above have been validated by rigorous research, while others have been shown consistently to help improve students' reading abilities in localized situations. There simply is not enough space to list all the strategies out there that have been proven effective; just know that the above strategies are very commonly cited ones that work in a variety of situations.

Prior Knowledge

Prior knowledge can be defined as all of an individual's prior experiences, learning, and development which precede his/her entering a specific learning situation or attempting to comprehend a specific text. Sometimes prior knowledge can be erroneous or incomplete. Obviously, if there are misconceptions in a child's prior knowledge, these must be corrected so that the child's overall comprehension skills can continue to progress. Prior knowledge of even kindergarteners includes their accumulated positive and negative experiences both in and out of school.

These might range from wonderful family travels, watching television, visiting museums and libraries, to visiting hospitals, prisons and surviving poverty. Whatever the prior knowledge that the child brings to the school setting, the independent reading and writing the child does in school immeasurably expands his/her prior knowledge and hence broadens his/her reading comprehension capabilities. Literary response skills are dependent on prior knowledge, schemata and background. Schemata (the plural of schema) are those structures which represent generic concepts stored in our memory. All readers, whether adults or children, who effectively comprehend text use both their schemata and prior knowledge PLUS the ideas from the printed text for reading comprehension, and graphic organizers help organize this information.

Graphic Organizers

Graphic organizers solidify in a chart format a visual relationship among various reading and writing ideas including: sequence, timelines, character traits, fact and opinion, main idea and details, differences and likenesses (generally done using a Venn diagram of interlocking circles, KWL Chart, and others). These charts and formats are essential for providing scaffolding for instruction through activating pertinent prior knowledge.

K-W-L Strategy is a graphic organizer strategy which activates children's prior knowledge and also helps them target their reading of expository texts. This focus is achieved through having the children reflect on three key questions.

Before the child read the expository passage:
"What do I ***K***now?" and
"What do I or we ***W***ant to find out?"

After the child has read the expository passage:
"What have I or we ***L***earned from the passage?"

What is excellent about this strategy, which is broadly used and easily implemented in almost any classroom, is that it is almost totally student- centered and powerfully focuses the children's attention on the actual reading of expository passages. The K-W-L strategy also helps the children prepare for a potential writing task.

When you first introduce the K-W-L strategy, allow sufficient time for the children to brainstorm what all of them in the class or small group actually know about the topic. The children should have a three-columned K-W-L worksheet template for their journals and there should be a chart up front to record the responses from class or group discussion. The children can write under each column in their own journal and should also help you with notations on the chart. This strategy enables the children to gain experience in note taking and keep a concrete record of new data and information they have gleaned from the passage about the topic.

Know	Want	Learn
In this box, the teacher or students list the information they already know about the topic to be discussed	In this box, the teacher or students list the questions they have about the topic, which may be answered through research or the activities already planned to be completed	In this box, the teacher or students list what information has been learned at the end of the teaching process. This becomes a reflective piece for both students and teachers and can even be used as a quick assessment for the teacher to ascertain all predetermined objectives were met.

Depending on the grade level of the participating children, you may also want to channel them into considering categories of information they hope to find out from the expository passage. For instance, they may be reading a book on animals to find out more about the animal's habitats during the winter or about the animal's mating habits.

When children are working on the middle-section (*W*ant) strategy sheet, give them a chance to share what they would like to learn further about the topic and help them to express it in question format.

K-W-L is useful and can even be introduced as early as grade 2 with extensive teacher support. It not only serves to support the children's comprehension of a particular expository text but also models for children a format for note taking.

Beyond note taking, when you want to introduce report writing, the K-W-L format provides excellent outlines and question introductions for at least three paragraphs of a report.

Cooper (2004) recommends this strategy for use with thematic units and with reading chapters in required science, social studies, or health text books.

In addition to its usefulness with thematic unit study, K-W-L is wonderful for providing you with a concrete format to assess how well children have absorbed pertinent new knowledge within the passage (by looking at the third *L*earn section). Ultimately it is hoped that students will learn to use this strategy, not only under explicit teacher direction with templates of K-W-L sheets but also on their own by informally writing questions they want to find out about in their journals and then going back to their own questions and answering them after reading.

Both English Language Learners and struggling readers can benefit from the structure and format of the K-W-L approach. It allows them to share their prior experiences and knowledge of the topics covered in the expository text through natural conversation. It provides them with a natural device for the teacher or tutor to customize and to scaffold instruction to meet their linguistic and experiential backgrounds. Through the discussion and sharing of other children's comments, struggling readers and children from ELL backgrounds have an opportunity to learn how to use questions to "walk through" and take notes on expository writing.

Highly proficient readers can do a comparative expository news event study between print accounts, e-news reportage, and broadcast media coverage. They can prepare charts and their own news mock-up to show the similarities and contrasts between what aspects of the event get covered in what media format. They may also want to write to actual reporters and editors from the different media to share their insights and see if these professionals are willing to respond.

Retelling

Retelling needs to be very clearly defined so that the readers do not think that you want them to spill the whole story back in the retelling. Children should be able to talk comfortably and fluently about the story they have just read. They should be able to tell the main things that have happened in the story.

When children retell a story, you need ways to help them assess their understanding. Ironically, you can use some of the same strategies that you might suggest to the children. These strategies include back cover reading, scanning the table of contents, looking at the pictures, and reading the book jacket.

If the children can explain how the story turned out and provide examples to support these explanations, try not to interrupt with too many questions.

Children can use the text of the book to reinforce what they are saying and they can even read from it if they wish. Remember that some children need to re-read the text twice and their re-reading if for enjoyment.

When you plan to use the retelling as a way of assessment, then set the following ground rules and make them clear to the children. Explain the purpose of the retelling to determine how well the children are reading at the outset of the conference.

You can record in their assessment notebooks what the children say by writing key phrases they use. Record just enough to indicate their understanding of the story. You should also try to analyze what the children have not comprehended from the text. If the accuracy rate with the text is below 95 percent, then the problem is at the word level, but if the accuracy rate for the text is above 95 per cent, the difficulty lies at the text level.

Inferencing

Inferencing is a process that involves the reader making a reasonable judgment based on the information given and engages children to literally construct meaning. You can develop and enhance this key skill in children with a mini lesson where you demonstrate this by reading an expository book aloud (i.e. one on skyscrapers for young children) and then demonstrate for them the following reading habits: looking for clues, reflecting on what the reader already knows about the topic, and using the clues to figure out what the author means/intends.

Main Idea

Identifying main ideas in an expository text can be improved when the children have an explicit strategy for identifying important information. They can make this strategy part of their everyday reading style, "walking" through the following exercises during guided reading sessions. Children should read the passage so that the topic is readily identifiable. It will be what most of the information is about.

Next they should be asked to be on the lookout for a sentence within the expository passage that summarizes the key information in the paragraph. Then the children should read the rest of the passage or excerpt in light of this information and also note which information in the paragraph is less important. The important information the children have identified in the paragraph can be used to formulate the author's main idea. The readers may even want to use some of the author's own language in stating that idea.

Monitoring

Monitoring means self-clarifying: As they read, the children often realize that what they are reading is not making sense. They then need a plan for making sense out of the excerpt. Cooper and other balanced literacy advocates have a stop and think strategy which they use with children. A child reflects, "Does this make sense to me?" When the child concludes that it does not, the child then either re-reads, reads ahead in the text, looks up unknown words or asks for help from the teacher.

What is important about monitoring is that some readers ask these questions and try these approaches without ever being explicitly taught them in school by a teacher. However, these strategies need to be explicitly modeled and practiced under the guidance of the teacher by most, if not all, child readers.

Discussing the Text

Discussion is an activity in which the children (and this activity works well from grades 3-6 and beyond) conclude a particular text. Among the prompts, the teacher-coach might suggest that the children focus on words of interest they encountered in the text. These can also be words that they heard if the text was read aloud. Children can be asked to share something funny or upsetting or unusual about the words they have read. Through this focus on children's response to words as the center of the discussion circle, peers become more interested in word study.

Small group or whole-class discussion stimulates thoughts about texts and gives students a larger picture of the impact of those texts. For example, teachers can strategically encourage students to discuss related concepts to the text. This helps students learn to consider texts within larger societal and social concepts, or teachers can encourage students to provide personal opinions in discussion. By listening to various students' opinions, this will help all students in a class to see the wide range of possible interpretations and thoughts regarding one text.

Furthermore, in the current teaching of literacy, reading, writing, thinking, listening, viewing, and discussing, are not viewed as separate activities or components of instruction, but rather as developing and being nurtured simultaneously and interactively.

Higher-Ordered Thinking Skills

Developing critical thinking skills in students is not as simple as developing other simpler skills. In fact, many teachers mistakenly believe that these skills can be taught out of context (i.e., they can be taught as skills in and of themselves). Good teachers, however, realize that critical thinking skills must be taught within the contexts of specific subject matter. For example, language arts teachers can teach critical thinking skills through novels; social studies teachers can teach critical thinking skills through primary source documents or current events; science teachers can teach critical thinking skills by having students develop hypotheses prior to conducting experiments.

First, let's start with definitions of the various types of critical thinking skills. **Analysis** is the systematic exploration of a concept, event, term, piece of writing, element of media, or any other complex item. Usually, people think of analysis as the exploration of the parts that make up a whole. For example, when someone analyzes a piece of literature, that person might focus on small pieces of the literature; yet, as they focus on the small pieces, they also call attention to the big picture and show how the small pieces create significance for the whole novel.

To carry this example further, if one were to analyze a novel, that person might investigate a particular character to determine how that character adds significance to the whole novel. In something more concrete like biology, one could analyze the findings of an experiment to see if the results might indicate significance for something even larger than the experiment itself. It is very easy to analyze political events, for example. A social studies teacher could ask students to analyze the events leading up to World War II: doing so would require that students look at the small pieces (e.g., smaller world events prior to World War II) and determine how those small pieces, when added up together, caused the war.

Next, let's consider **synthesis**. Synthesis is usually thought of to be the opposite of analysis. In analysis, we take a whole and break it up into pieces and look at the pieces. With synthesis, we take different things and make them one whole thing. For example, a language arts teacher could ask students to synthesize two works of distinct literature. Let's say that we take *The Scarlett Letter* and *The Crucible*, two works both featuring life during Puritanical America, written about one century apart. A student could synthesize the two works and come to conclusions about Puritanical life. An Art teacher could ask students to synthesize two paintings from the Impressionist era and come to conclusions about the features that distinguish that style of art.

Finally, **evaluation** involves making judgments. Whereas analysis and synthesis seek answers and hypotheses based on investigations, evaluation seeks opinions. For example, a social studies teacher could ask students to evaluate the quality of Richard Nixon's resignation speech. To do so, they would judge whether or not they felt it was good (according to some set of standards). In contrast, analysis would keep judgment out of the assignment: it would have students focus possibly on the structure of the speech (i.e., Does an argument move from emotional to logical?). When evaluating a speech, a piece of literature, a movie, or a work of art, we seek to determine whether one thinks it is good or not. But, keep in mind, teaching good evaluation skills requires not just that students learn how to determine whether something is good or not—it requires that they learn how to support their evaluations. So, if a student claims that Nixon's speech was effective in what the President intended the speech to do, the student would need to explain how this is so. Notice that evaluation will probably utilize the skills of analysis and/or synthesis, but that the purpose is ultimately different.

Encouraging Independent Critical Thinking

Since most teachers want their educational objectives to use higher level thinking skills, teachers need to direct students to these higher levels on the taxonomy. Questioning is an effective tool to build up students to these higher levels. Low order questions are useful to begin the process. They insure the student is focused on the required information and understands what needs to be included in the thinking process. For example, if the objective is for students to be able to read and understand the story "Goldilocks and the Three Bears," the teacher may wish to start with low order questions (i.e., "What are some things Goldilocks did while in the bears home?" [Knowledge] or "Why didn't Goldilocks like the Papa Bear's chair?" [Analysis]).

Through a series of questions, the teacher can move the students up the taxonomy. (For example, "If Goldilocks had come to your house, what are some things she may have used?" [Application], "How might the story differed if Goldilocks had visited the three fishes?" [Synthesis], or "Do you think Goldilocks was good or bad? Why?" [Evaluation]). The teacher through questioning can control the thinking process of the class. As students become more involved in the discussion they are systematically being lead to higher level thinking.

To develop a critical-thinking approach to the world, children need to know enough about valid and invalid reasoning to ask questions. Bringing into the classroom speeches or essays that demonstrate both valid and invalid examples can be useful in helping students develop the ability to question the reasoning of others. These will be published writers or televised speakers, so they can see that they are able even to question ideas that are accepted by some adults and talk about what is wrong in the thinking of those apparently successful communicators.

If the teacher stays right on the cutting edge of children's experience, they will become more and more curious about what is out there in the world that they don't know about. A lesson on a particular country or even a tribe in the world that the children may not even know exists that will use various kinds of media to reveal to them what life is like there for children their own age is a good way to introduce the world out there. In such a presentation, positive aspects of the lives of those "other" children should be included. Perhaps a correspondence with a village could be developed. It's good for children, some of whom may not live very high on the social scale in this country, to know what the rest of the world is like, and in so doing, develop an independent curiosity to know more.

In general, critical thinking skills should be taught through assignments, activities, lessons, and discussions that cause students to think on their own. While teachers can and should provide students with the tools to think critically, they will ultimately become critical thinkers if they have to use those tools themselves. But, this one last point cannot be taken lightly: Teachers must provide students the tools to evaluate, analyze, and synthesize.

Let's take political speeches as an example. Students will be better analyzers, synthesizers, and evaluators if they understand some of the basics of political speeches. Therefore, a teacher might introduce concepts such as rhetoric, style, persona, audience, diction, imagery, and tone. The best way to introduce these concepts would be to provide students with multiple, good examples of these things. Once they are familiar with these critical tools, students will be in a better place to apply them individually to political speeches—and then be able to analyze, synthesize, and evaluate political speeches on their own.

Skill 10.5 Demonstrate knowledge of methods for helping students interpret written directions

How does one get from here to there, from kindergarten to graduate school or to-a trade school? The answer of course is by one step at a time, by carefully organizing one's courses of action, each phase building on the previous step and leading to the next.

Similarly, when taking a test you are asked to follow written instructions or directions the examiner wants to see how you manage your answer to the exam question. How do you organize your answer logically? How do you support your conclusions? How well connected are your ideas and the support you bring to your argument?

Look at how the writer does these tasks in the following essay:

> Parenting Classes
>
> Someone once said that the two most difficult jobs in the world—voting and being a parent—are given to rank amateurs. The consequences of this inequity are voter apathy and inept parenting leading to, on the one hand, an apparent failure of the democratic process and, on the other hand, misbehaving and misguided children.
>
> The antidote for the first problem is in place in most school systems. Classes in history, civics, history, government, and student government provide a kind of "hands on" training in becoming an active member of society so that the step from student hood to citizenship is clear and expected.

On the other hand, most school systems in the past have avoided or given only lip service to the issue of parenting and parenting skills. The moral issue of illegitimate births aside, the reality of the world is that each year there are large numbers of children born to unwed parents who have had little, or no, training in child rearing.

What was done on the farm in the past is irrelevant here: the farm is gone and/or has been replaced by the inner city, and the pressing issue is how to train uneducated new parents in the child rearing tasks before them. Other issues are secondary to the immediate needs of newborns and their futures. And it is in their futures that the quality of life for all of us is found.

Thus, while we can debate this issue all we wish, we cannot responsibly ignore that uneducated parents need to be educated in the tasks before them, and it is clear that the best way to do this is in the school system, where these new parents are already learning how to be responsible citizens in the civics and other classes currently in place.

Notice how the writer moves sequentially from one idea to the next, maintaining throughout the parallel of citizenship and parenthood, from the opening quotation, paragraph by paragraph to the concluding sentence. Each idea is developed from the preceding idea, and each new idea refers to the preceding ideas, and at no point do related, but irrelevant issues sidetrack the writer.

COMPETENCY 11.0 UNDERSTAND THE APPLICATION OF WRITING SKILLS TO CLASSROOM INSTRUCTION

Skill 11.1 Demonstrate an awareness of techniques for helping students generate and organize ideas for writing (e.g., outlines, freewriting, graphic organizers)

Prewriting may include clustering, listing, brainstorming, mapping, free writing, and charting. Providing many ways for students to develop their ideas on a topic will increase their chances for success.

Remind students that as they prewrite they need to consider their audience. Prewriting strategies assist students in a variety of ways. Listed below are the most common prewriting strategies students can use to explore, plan and write on a topic. Remember when teaching these strategies that not all prewriting must eventually produce a finished piece of writing. In fact, in the initial lesson of teaching prewriting strategies, it might be more effective to have students practice prewriting strategies without the pressure of having to write a finished product.

- Keep an idea book so that they can jot down ideas that come to mind.
- Write in a daily journal.
- Write down whatever comes to mind; this is called free writing. Students do not stop to make corrections or interrupt the flow of ideas.

A variation of this technique is focused free writing—writing on a specific topic—to prepare for an essay.

- Make a list of all ideas connected with their topic; this is called brainstorming
- Make sure students know that this technique works best when they let their mind work freely. After completing the list, students should analyze the list to see if a pattern or way to group the ideas
- Ask the questions Who? What? When? Where? When? and How? Help the writer approach a topic from several perspectives
- Create a visual map on paper to gather ideas. Cluster circles and lines to show connections between ideas. Students should try to identify the relationship that exists between their ideas. If they cannot see the relationships, have them pair up, exchange papers and have their partners look for some related ideas
- Observe details of sight, hearing, taste, touch, and taste
- Visualize by making mental images of something and write down the details in a list

Before actually writing, you'll need to generate content and to develop a writing plan. Three prewriting techniques that can be helpful are brainstorming, questioning, and clustering.

Brainstorming—When brainstorming, quickly create a list of words and ideas that are connected to the topic. Let your mind roam free to generate as many relevant ideas as possible in a few minutes. For example, on the topic of computers you may write

> computer - modern invention
> types - personal computers, micro-chips in calculators and watches
> wonder - acts like an electronic brain
> uses - science, medicine, offices, homes, schools
> problems- too much reliance; the machines aren't perfect

This list could help you focus on the topic and states the points you could develop in the body paragraphs. The brainstorming list keeps you on track and is well worth the few minutes it takes to jot down the ideas. While you haven't ordered the ideas, seeing them on paper is an important step.

Questioning—Questioning helps you focus as you mentally ask a series of exploratory questions about the topic. You may use the most basic questions: who, what, where, when, why, and how.

"**What** is my subject?"
[computers]

"**What** types of computers are there?"
[personal computers, micro-chip computers]

"**Why** have computers been a positive invention?"
[act like electronic brains in machinery and equipment; help solve complex scientific problems]

"**How** have computers been a positive invention?"
[used to make improvements in:

- science (space exploration, moon landings)
- medicine (MRIs, CAT scans, surgical tools, research models)
- business (PCs, FAX, telephone equipment)
- education (computer programs for math, languages, science, social studies), and
- personal use (family budgets, tax programs, healthy diet plans)

"**How** can **I** show that computers are good?"
[citing numerous examples]

"**What** problems do I see with computers?"
[too much reliance; not yet perfect.]

"**What** personal experiences would help me develop examples to respond to this topic?
[my own experiences using computers]

Of course, you may not have time to write out the questions completely. You might just write the words *who, what, where, why, how* and the major points next to each. An abbreviated list might look as follows:

What—computers/modern wonder/making life better

How—through technological improvements: lasers, calculators, CAT scans.

Where—in science and space exploration, medicine, schools, offices
In a few moments, your questions should help you to focus on the topic and to generate interesting ideas and points to make in the essay. Later in the writing process, you can look back at the list to be sure you've made the key points you intended.

Clustering—Some visual thinkers find clustering an effective prewriting method. When clustering, you draw a box in the center of your paper and write your topic within that box. Then you draw lines from the center box and connect it to small satellite boxes that contain related ideas. Note the cluster below on computers:

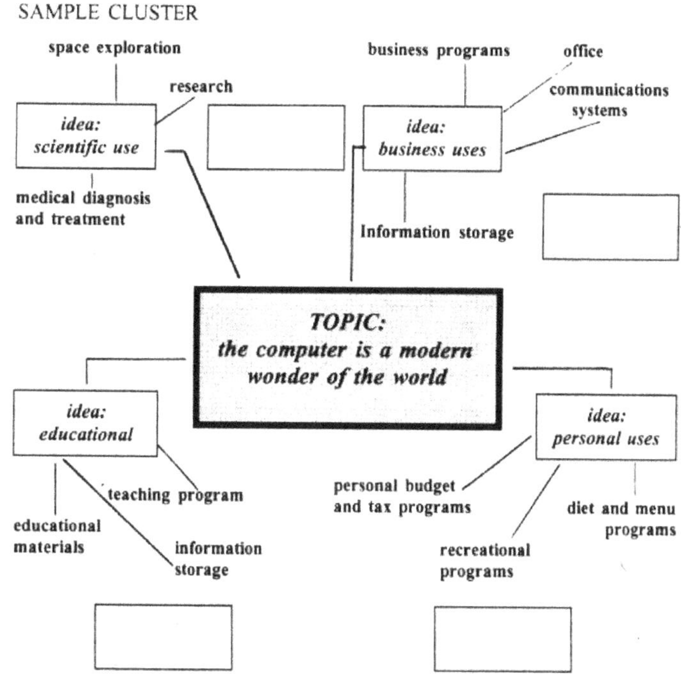

VISUAL ORGANIZER: GIVING REASONS

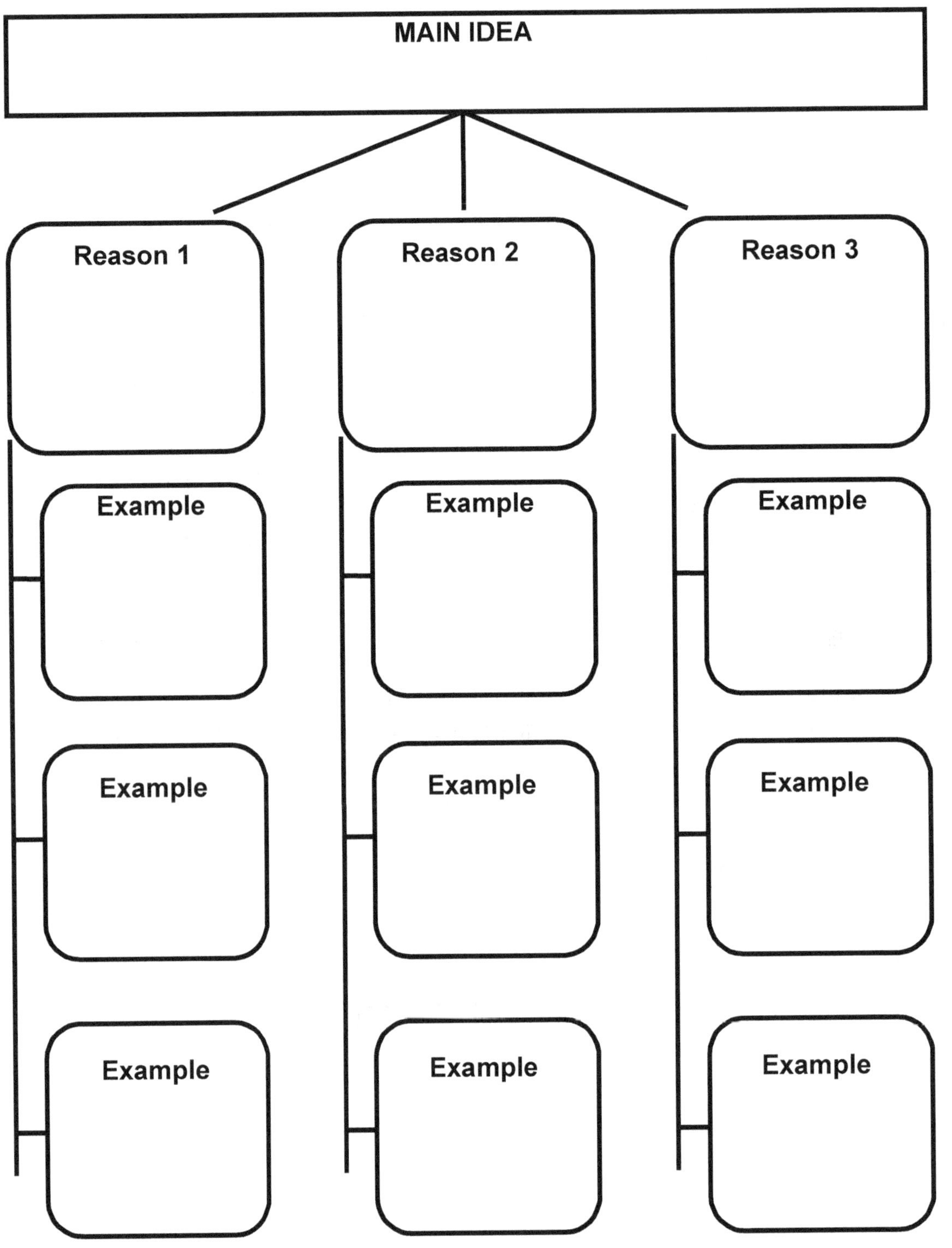

VISUAL ORGANIZER: GIVING INFORMATION

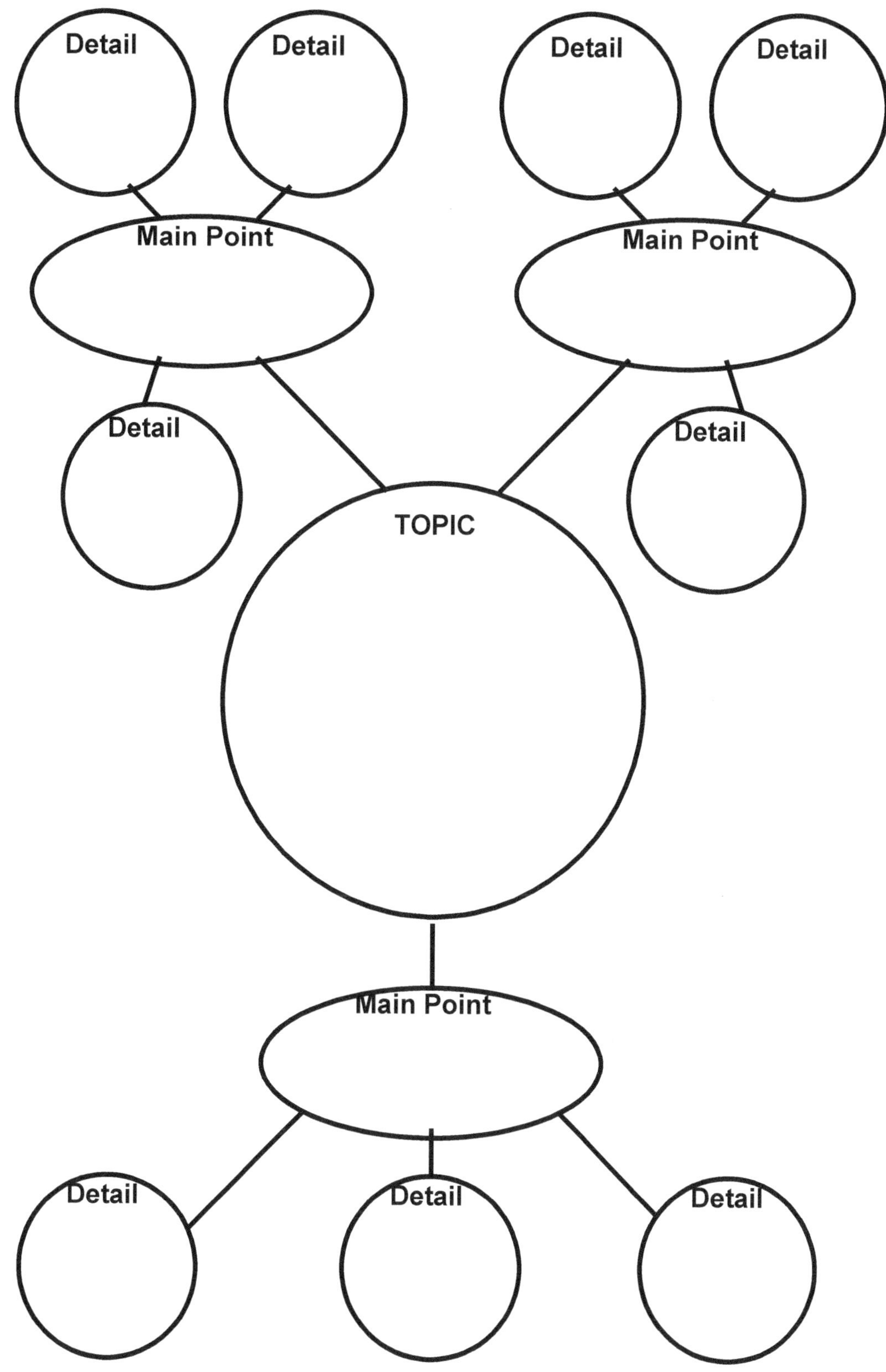

After focusing on the topic and generating your ideas, form your thesis, which is the controlling idea of your essay. The thesis is your general statement to the reader that expresses your point of view and guides your essay's purpose and scope. The thesis should allow you either to explain your subject or to take an arguable position about it. A strong thesis statement is neither too narrow nor too broad.

Subject and Assertion of the Thesis

From the analysis of the general topic, you consider the topic in terms of its two parts, the *subject* and the *assertion*. On the exam, your thesis or viewpoint on a particular topic is stated in two important points:

> the **subject** of the paper and the **assertion** about the subject.

The **subject of the thesis** relates directly to the topic prompt but expresses the specific area you have chosen to discuss. (Remember the exam topic will be general and will allow you to choose a particular subject related to the topic). For example, the computer is one modern invention.

The **assertion of the thesis** is your viewpoint, or opinion, about the subject. The assertion provides the motive or purpose for your essay, and it may be an arguable point or one that explains or illustrates a point of view.

For example, you may present an argument for or against a particular issue. You may contrast two people, objects, or methods to show that one is better than the other. You may analyze a situation in all aspects and make recommendations for improvement. You may assert that a law or policy should be adopted, changed or abandoned. You may also, as in the computer example, explain to your reader that a situation or condition exists; rather than argue a viewpoint, you would use examples to illustrate your assertion about the essay's subject.

Specifically, the **subject** of Topic A is *the computer*. The **assertion** is that *it is a modern wonder that has improved our lives and that we rely on*. Now you quickly have created a workable thesis in a few moments:

> *The computer is a modern wonder of the world that has improved our lives and that we have come to rely on.*

Guidelines for Writing Thesis Statements

The following guidelines are not a formula for writing thesis statements but rather are general strategies for making your thesis statement clearer and more effective.

1. State a *particular point* of *view* about the topic with both a *subject* and an *assertion.* The thesis should give the essay purpose and scope and thus provide the reader a guide. If the thesis is vague, your essay may be undeveloped because you do not have an idea to assert or a point to explain. Weak thesis statements are often framed as facts, questions or announcements:

    a. Avoid a fact statement as a thesis. While a fact statement may provide a subject, it generally does not include a point of view about the subject that provides the basis for an extended discussion.

        Example: *Recycling saved our community over $10,000 last year.* This fact statement provides a detail, *not* a point of view. Such a detail might be found within an essay, but it does not state a point of view.

    b. Avoid framing the thesis as a vague question. In many cases, rhetorical questions do not provide a clear point of view for an extended essay.

        Example: *How do people recycle?* This question neither asserts a point of view nor helps the reader to understand the essay's purpose and scope.

    c. Avoid the "announcer" topic sentence that merely states the topic you will discuss

        Example: I *will discuss ways to recycle.* This sentence states the subject, but the scope of the essay is only suggested. Again, this statement does not assert a viewpoint that guides the essay's purpose. It merely "announces" that the writer will write about the topic.

2. Start with a workable thesis. You might revise your thesis as you begin writing and discover your own point of view.

3. If feasible and appropriate, perhaps state the thesis in multi-point form, expressing the scope of the essay. By stating the points in parallel form, you clearly lay out the essay's plan for the reader.

    Example: *To improve the environment, we can recycle our trash, elect politicians who see the environment as a priority, and support lobbying groups who work for environmental protection.*

4. Because of the exam time limit, place your thesis in the first paragraph to key the reader to the essay's main idea.

Creating a Working Outline

A good thesis gives structure to your essay and helps focus your thoughts. When forming your thesis, look at your prewriting strategy — brainstorming, questioning, or clustering. Then decide quickly which two or three major areas you'll discuss. Remember, you must limit *the scope* of the paper because of the time factor.

The **outline** lists those main areas or points as topics for each paragraph. Looking at the prewriting cluster on computers, you might choose several areas in which computers help us, for example in science and medicine, business, and education. You might also consider people's reliance on this "wonder" and include at least one paragraph about this reliance. A formal outline for this essay might look like the one below:

I. Introduction and thesis

II. Computers used in science and medicine

III. Computers used in business

IV. Computers used in education

V. People's reliance on computers

VI. Conclusion

Under time pressure, however, you may use a shorter organizational plan, such as abbreviated key words in a list. For example

1. intro: wonders of the computer
2. science
3. med
4. schools
5. business
6. conclusion

a. intro: wonders of computers - science
b. in the space industry
c. in medical technology
d. conclusion

Developing the Essay

With a working thesis and outline, you can begin writing the essay. The essay should be in three main sections:

1. The introduction sets up the essay and leads to the thesis statement.

2. The body paragraphs are developed with concrete information leading from the topic sentences.

3. The conclusion ties the essay together.

Skill 11.2 Demonstrate knowledge of methods for monitoring student writing and identify basic problems students may be having in their written work

Viewing writing as a process allows teachers and students to see the writing classroom as a cooperative workshop where students and teachers encourage and support each other in each writing endeavor. Listed below are some techniques that help teachers to facilitate and create a supportive classroom environment.

Learn more about
Re-establishing Reading and Writing Workshops
http://curriculum.dpsk12.org/Planning_guides/Literacy/7/7_Addenda.pdf

1. Create peer response/support groups that are working on similar writing assignments. The members help each other in all stages of the writing process—from prewriting, writing, revising, editing, and publishing.

2. Provide several prompts to give students the freedom to write on a topic of their own. Writing should be generated out of personal experience and students should be introduced to in-class journals. One effective way to get into writing is to let them write often and freely about their own lives, without having to worry about grades or evaluation.

3. Respond in the form of a question whenever possible. Teacher/facilitator should respond non-critically and use positive, supportive language.

4. Respond to formal writing acknowledging the student's strengths and focusing on the composition skills demonstrated by the writing. A response should encourage the student by offering praise for what the student has done well. Give the student a focus for revision and demonstrate that the process of revision has applications in many other writing situations.

5. Provide students with readers' checklists so that students can write observational critiques of others' drafts, and then they can revise their own papers at home using the checklists as a guide.

6. Pair students so that they can give and receive responses. Pairing students keeps them aware of the role of an audience in the composing process and in evaluating stylistic effects.

7. Focus critical comments on aspects of the writing that can be observed in the writing. Comments like "I noticed you use the word 'is' frequently" will be more helpful than "Your introduction is dull" and will not demoralize the writer.

8. Provide the group with a series of questions to guide them through the group writing sessions.

Skill 11.3 Recognize effective techniques for helping students edit and proofread their writing (e.g., correcting errors in grammar and spelling)

Revision is probably the most important step for the writer in the writing process. Here, students examine their work and make changes in wording, details, and ideas. So many times, students write a draft and then feel they're done. On the contrary, students must be encouraged to develop, change, and enhance their writing as they go, as well as once they've completed a draft.

Many teachers introduce Writer's Workshop to their students to maximize learning about the writing process. Writer's Workshops vary across classrooms, but the main idea is for students to become comfortable with the writing process to produce written work. A basic Writer's Workshop will include a block of classroom time committed to writing various projects (i.e., narratives, memoirs, book summaries, fiction, or book reports). Students use this time to write, meet with others to review/edit writing, make comments on writing, revise their own work, proofread, meet with the teacher, and publish their work.

Teachers who facilitate effective Writer's Workshops are able to meet with students one at a time and can guide that student in individual writing needs. This approach allows the teacher to differentiate instruction for each student's writing level. Viewing writing as a process allows teachers and students to see the writing classroom as a cooperative place where students and teachers encourage and support each other in each writing endeavor. Listed below are some techniques that help teachers to facilitate and create a supportive classroom environment.

Responding to Non-Graded Writing (Formative)

- Avoid using a red pen. Whenever possible use a #2 pencil.
- Explain the criteria that will be used for assessment in advance.
- Read the writing once while asking the question, "Is the student's response appropriate for the assignment?"
- Reread and make note at the end whether the student met the objective of the writing task.
- Responses should be non-critical and use supportive and encouraging language.

- Resist writing on or over the student's writing.
- Highlight the ideas you wish to emphasize, question, or verify.
- Encourage your students to take risks.

Responding to and Evaluating Graded Writing (Summative)

- Ask students to submit prewriting and rough-draft materials including all revisions with their final draft.
- For the first reading, use a holistic method, examining the work as a whole.
- When reading the draft for the second time, assess it using the standards previously established.
- Responses to the writing should be written in the margin and should use supportive language.
- Make sure you address the process as well as the product. It is important that students value the learning process as well as the final product.
- After scanning the piece a third time, write final comments at the end of the draft.

Skill 11.4 Demonstrate the ability to identify appropriate reference materials (e.g., dictionaries, library resources, the Internet) as well as effective techniques for helping students use them

In our increasingly knowledge-based world, educators have found that it is not good enough to simply teach students factual information. The information teachers pass on to students is inherently going to be limited and soon out-dated. It is said that the body of knowledge in most academic fields doubles within a matter of years. That being said, we can assume that the factual information students do get in the classroom will not necessarily represent the most current, accurate information available.

Because of the rapidly accelerating amount of information available, educators cannot shirk the responsibility of not teaching students how to access sources of information. References sources can be of great value, and by teaching students how to access these first, they will later have skills that will help them access more in-depth databases and sources of information.

In all, reference tools are highly valuable for students. Surprisingly, it takes a very long time for students to become competent with most reference tools, but the effort and time is definitely worth it.

Encyclopedias are reference materials that appear in book or electronic form. Encyclopedias can be considered general or specific. General encyclopedias peripherally cover most fields of knowledge; specific encyclopedias cover a smaller amount of material in greater depth. Encyclopedias are good first sources of information for students. While their total scope is limited, they can provide a quick introduction to topics so that students can get familiar with the topics before exploring the topics in greater depth.

Almanacs provide statistical information on various topics. Typically, these references are rather specific. They often cover a specific period of time. One famous example is the *Farmer's Almanac*. This annual publication summarizes, among many other things, weather conditions for the previous year.

Bibliographies contain references for further research. Bibliographies are usually organized topically. They help point people to the in-depth resources they will need for a complete view of a topic.

Databases, typically all electronic now, are collections of material on specific topics. For example, teachers can go online and find many databases of science articles for students in a variety of topics.

Atlases are visual representations of geographic areas. Often, they serve different functions. Some atlases demonstrate geologic attributes while others emphasize populations of various areas.

Periodical guides categorize articles and special editions of journals and magazines to help archive and organize the vast amount of material that is put in periodicals each year.

Dictionaries are useful for spelling, writing, and reading. It is very important to initially expose and habituate students to enjoy using the dictionary. Cooper (2004) suggests that the following be kept in mind as the teacher of grades K-6 introduces and then habituates children in what is hoped to be a lifelong fascination with the dictionary and vocabulary acquisition.

- Requesting or suggesting that children look up a word in the dictionary should be an invitation to a wonderful exploration, not a punishment or busy work that has no reference to their current reading assignment.

- Model the correct way to use the dictionary for children even as late as the third through sixth grade. Many have never been taught proper dictionary skills. Demonstrate to the children that as an adult readers and writers, they routinely and happily use the dictionary and learn new information that make them better at reading and writing.

- Do not routinely require children to look up every new spelling word in the dictionary

Some experts believe in beginning dictionary study as early as kindergarten, and this is now very possible because of the proliferation of lush picture dictionaries which can be introduced at that grade level. These experts also suggest that children not only look at these picture dictionaries but also begin to make dictionaries of their own at this grade level filled with pictures and beginning words. As children join the circle of lexicographers, they will begin to see themselves as compilers and users of dictionaries. Of course, this will support their ongoing vocabulary development.

On early grade levels, use of the dictionary can nicely complement the children's mastery of the alphabet. They should be given whole class and small group practice in locating words.

As the children progress with their phonetic skills, the dictionary can be used to show them phonetic respelling using the pronunciation key.

Older children in grades 3 and beyond need explicit teacher demonstrations and practice in use of guide words. They also need to begin to learn about the hierarchies of various word meanings. In the upper grades, children should also explore using special content dictionaries and glossaries in the backs of their books.

Primary and Secondary Sources

The resources used to support a piece of writing can be divided into two major groups: **primary** sources and **secondary** sources.

Primary sources are works, records, and the like that were created during the period being studied or immediately after it. Secondary sources are works written significantly after the period being studied and based upon primary sources. Primary sources are the basic materials that provide raw data and information. Secondary sources are the works that contain the explications of, and judgments on, this primary material.

Primary sources include the following kinds of materials:

- Documents that reflect the immediate, everyday concerns of people: memoranda, bills, deeds, charters, newspaper reports, pamphlets, graffiti, popular writings, journals or diaries, records of decision-making bodies, letters, receipts, snapshots, and others.

- Theoretical writings which reflect care and consideration in composition and an attempt to convince or persuade. The topic will generally be deeper and more pervasive values than is the case with "immediate" documents. These may include newspaper or magazine editorials, sermons, political speeches, or philosophical writings.
- Narrative accounts of events, ideas, and trends written with intentionality by someone contemporary with the events described.
- Statistical data, although statistics may be misleading.
- Literature and nonverbal materials, novels, stories, poetry and essays from the period, as well as coins, archaeological artifacts, and art produced during the period.

In **primary research**, selecting a topic and setting up an outline for research information precedes using the secondary research of both print and electronic resources. Using conceptual Venn diagrams to center the topic and brainstorm the peripheral information pertaining to the topic clarifies the purpose of the research.

Secondary sources include the following kinds of materials:

- Books written on the basis of primary materials about the period of time.
- Books written on the basis of primary materials about persons who played a major role in the events under consideration.
- Books and articles written on the basis of primary materials about the culture, the social norms, the language, and the values of the period.
- Quotations from primary sources.
- Statistical data on the period.
- The conclusions and inferences of other historians.
- Multiple interpretations of the ethos of the time.

Guidelines for the use of secondary sources:

1. Do not rely upon only a single secondary source.
2. Check facts and interpretations against primary sources whenever possible.
3. Do not accept the conclusions of other historians uncritically.
4. Place greatest reliance on secondary sources created by the best and most respected scholars.
5. Do not use the inferences of other scholars as if they were facts.
6. Ensure that you recognize any bias the writer brings to his/her interpretation of history.
7. Understand the primary point of the book as a basis for evaluating the value of the material presented in it to your questions.

There are two aspects of the **secondary research**: using print sources and using electronic research tools.

Print sources provide guides on locations for specific or general information resources. Libraries have floors or designated areas dedicated to the collection of encyclopedias, specific resource manuals, card catalogs, and periodical indexes that will provide information on the projected topic.

Locating information for research projects and compiling research sources using both print and electronic resources are vital in the construct of written documents. The resources that are available in today's school communities include a large database of Internet resources and World Wide Web access that provides individual navigation for print and electronic information. Research sources include looking at traditional commercial databases and using The Electronic Library to print and cite a diversity of informational resources.

The vital aspect of the research process includes learning to analyze the applicability and validity of the massive amounts of accessible information in cyberspace. Verifying and evaluating electronic resources are part of the process of sorting through the downloaded hardcopies or scrolling through the electronic databases. In using a diversity of research sources, the user must be able to discern authentic sources of information from the mass collections of websites and information databases.

Electronic research tools includes a listing of the latest and most effective search engines like Goggle, Microsoft, AOL, Infotrac, and Yahoo to find the topic of research, along with peripheral support information. Electronic databases that contain extensive resources will provide the user with selecting resources, choosing effective keywords, and constructing search strategies. The world of electronic research opens up a global library of resources for both print and electronic information.

The major online services such as Microsoft, Prodigy, and CompuServe provide users with assess information of specialized information that is either free or one that has a minimal charge assessed for that specific service or website. Online resources teach effective ways to bookmark sites of interest and how to cut and paste relevant information onto word documents for citation and reference.

Bookmarking favorite Internet searches that contain correct sources for reference can save a lot of research time. On AOL, book marking is known as favorites and with one click of the mouse, a user can type in the email address on the browser's location bar and create instant access to that location. Netscape uses the terminology of "bookmarks" to save browser locations for future research.

Online search engines and web portals create avenues of navigating the World Wide Web portals provide linkages to other websites and are typically subdivided into other categories for searching. Portals are also specific to certain audience interests that index parts of the web. Search engines can provide additional strategic site searches.

Questions for Analyzing Sources

To determine the authenticity or credibility of your sources, consider these questions:

Learn more about **Assessing the Credibility of Online Sources**
http://www.webcredible.co.uk/user-friendly-resources/web-credibility/assessing-credibility-online-sources.shtml

1. Who created the source and why? Was it created through a spur-of-the-moment act, a routine transaction, or a thoughtful, deliberate process?

2. Did the recorder have firsthand knowledge of the event? Or, did the recorder report what others saw and heard?

3. Was the recorder a neutral party, or did the recorder have opinions or interests that might have influenced what was recorded?

4. Did the recorder produce the source for personal use, for one or more individuals, or for a large audience?

5. Was the source meant to be public or private?

6. Did the recorder wish to inform or persuade others? (Check the words in the source. The words may tell you whether the recorder was trying to be objective or persuasive.) Did the recorder have reasons to be honest or dishonest?

7. Was the information recorded during the event, immediately after the event, or after some lapse of time? How large a lapse of time?

COMPETENCY 12.0 UNDERSTAND APPLICATION OF MATHEMATICS SKILLS TO CLASSROOM INSTRUCTION

Skill 12.1 Demonstrate the ability to relate mathematics to everyday situations

See Competencies 7.0 and 8.0.

Skill 12.2 Identify and correcting basic errors in addition, subtraction, multiplication, and division

The following are some possible types of errors in mathematical explanations:

- Information not appropriate or extraneous to the explanation
- Misuse of mathematical terms
- Inappropriate strategy for solving the problem
- Inappropriate or unexplained diagram
- Incomplete argument
- Incorrect labels or descriptions
- Key elements of the strategy are missing
- Algorithms incorrectly executed
- Words do not reflect the problem
- Process cannot be identified

See also Skill 7.1.

Skill 12.3 Demonstrate knowledge of techniques for helping students use instructional resources (e.g., math manipulative materials, rulers, money, charts, graphs, calculators) to support mathematical learning

Successful math teachers introduce their students to multiple problem solving strategies and create a classroom environment where free thought and experimentation are encouraged. Teachers can promote problem solving by allowing multiple attempts at problems, giving credit for reworking test or homework problems, and encouraging the sharing of ideas through class discussion. There are several specific problem solving skills with which teachers should be familiar.

The **guess-and-check** strategy calls for students to make an initial guess at the solution, check the answer, and use the outcome of to guide the next guess. With each successive guess, the student should get closer to the correct answer. Constructing a table from the guesses can help organize the data.

Example: There are 100 coins in a jar. 10 are dimes. The rest are pennies and nickels. There are twice as many pennies as nickels. How many pennies and nickels are in the jar?

There are 90 total nickels and pennies in the jar (100 coins – 10 dimes).

There are twice as many pennies as nickels. Make guesses that fulfill the criteria and adjust based on the answer found. Continue until we find the correct answer, 60 pennies and 30 nickels.

Number of Pennies	Number of Nickels	Total Number of Pennies and Nickels
40	20	60
80	40	120
70	35	105
60	30	90

When solving a problem where the final result and the steps to reach the result are given, students must **work backwards** to determine what the starting point must have been.

Example: John subtracted seven from his age, and divided the result by 3. The final result was 4. What is John's age?

Work backward by reversing the operations.
4 x 3 = 12;
12 + 7 = 19
John is 19 years old.

Drawing pictures or diagrams can sometimes help to make relationships in a problem clearer.

Example: In a women's marathon, the first five finishers in some order were Frieda, Polly, Christa, Betty, and Dora. Frieda finished seven seconds before Christa. Polly finished six seconds after Betty. Dora finished eight seconds after Betty. Christa finished two seconds before Polly. In what order did the women finish the race?

Drawing a picture or diagram will help us see the answer easily.

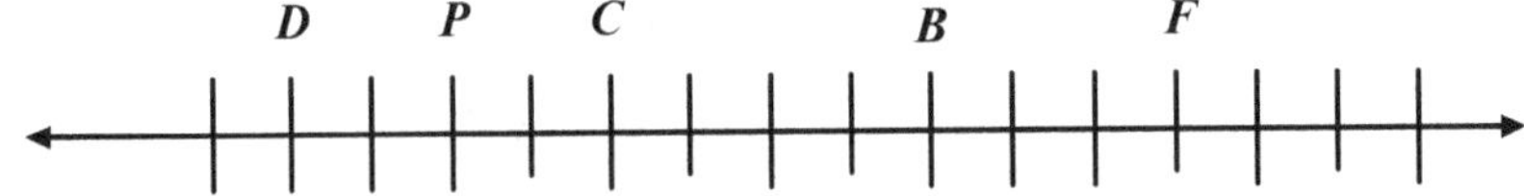

From the diagram, we can see that the women finished in the following order: 1st – Frieda, 2nd – Betty, 3rd – Christa, 4th – Polly, and 5th – Dora.

Sometimes, using a model is the best way to see the solution to a problem, as in the case of fraction multiplication.

For example: Model $\frac{5}{6} \times \frac{2}{3}$.

Draw a rectangle. Divide it vertically into 6 equal sections (the denominator of the first number.)

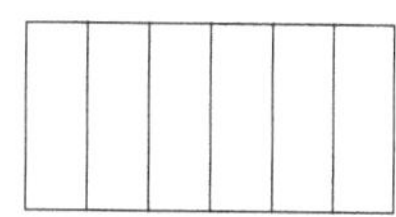

Divide the rectangle horizontally into 3 equal sections (the denominator of the second number).

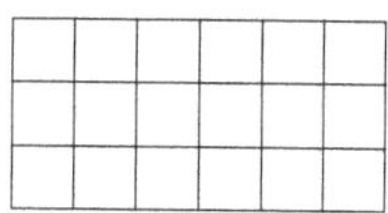

Color in a number of vertical strips equal to the numerator of the first number.

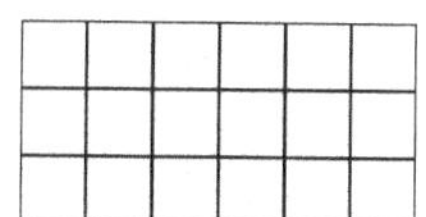

Use a different color to shade a number of horizontal strips equal to the numerator of the second number.

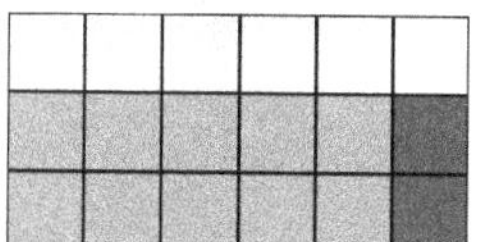

By describing the area where both colors overlap, we have the product of the two fractions: $\frac{10}{18}$.

SAMPLE TEST: INSTRUCTIONAL SUPPORT RATIONALES

1. **The major difference between phonemic and phonological awareness is: (Skill 10.1, Rigorous)**

   A. One deals with a series of discrete sounds and sound spelling relationships.
   B. One is involved with teaching and learning alliteration and rhymes.
   C. Phonemic awareness is a specific type phonological awareness that deals with separate phonemes within a given word.
   D. Phonological awareness is associated with printed words.

2. **All of the following are true about phonological awareness EXCEPT: (Skill 10.1, Average Rigor)**

   A. It may involve print.
   B. It is a prerequisite for spelling and phonics.
   C. Activities can be done by the children with their eyes closed.
   D. Starts before letter recognition is taught.

3. **The best way for a primary grade teacher to model directionality and one to one word matching would be: (Skill 10.1, Easy)**

   A. Using a regular library or classroom text book.
   B. Using her own person reading book.
   C. Using a big book.
   D. Using a book dummy.

4. **To decode is to: (Skill 10.1, Easy)**

   A. Construct meaning.
   B. Sound out a printed sequence of letters.
   C. Use a special code to decipher a message.
   D. None of the above.

5. **The word "bat" is a ___word for "batter-up": (Skill 10.1, Easy)**

   A. Suffix.
   B. Prefix.
   C. Root word.
   D. Inflectional ending.

6. **"Self correct" in reading means: (Skill 10.2, Average Rigor)**

   A. The teacher corrects on the record the errors the child makes.
   B. The child goes back and corrects errors made in a running record.
   C. The reading specialist teaches this to the child.
   D. a and

7. **How could a KWL chart be used in instruction? (Skill 10.3, Rigorous)**

   A. To motivate students to do a research paper
   B. To assess prior knowledge of the students
   C. To assist in teaching skills
   D. To put events in sequential order

8. **Julia has been hired to work in a school that serves a local public housing project. She is working with kindergarten children and has been asked to focus on shared reading. She selects: (Skill 10.4, Rigorous)**

   A. Chapter books.
   B. Riddle books.
   C. Alphabet books.
   D. Wordless picture books.

9. **A teacher has taught his students several strategies to monitor their reading comprehension. These strategies include identifying where in the passage they are having difficulty, identifying what the difficulty is, and restating the difficult sentence or passage in their own words. These strategies are examples of: (Skill 10.4, Rigorous)**

   A. graphic and semantic organizers
   B. metacognition
   C. recognizing story structure
   D. summarizing

10. **Asking a child if what he or she has read makes sense to him or her, is prompting the child to use: (Skill 10.4, Average Rigor)**

    A. Phonics cues.
    B. Syntactic cues.
    C. Semantic cues.
    D. Prior knowledge.

11. **When you ask a child, if what he or she has just read "sounds right" to him or her, you are trying to get that child to use: (Skill 10.4, Average Rigor)**

    A. Phonics cues.
    B. Syntactic cues.
    C. Semantic cues.
    D. Prior knowledge.

12. As part of study about the agricultural products of their state, children have identified 22 different types of apples produced in the state. They can use a _______to compare and contrast these different types of apples: (Skill 10.4, Average Rigor)

A. Word web.
B. Semantic map.
C. Semantic features analysis grid.
D. All of the above.

13. To help children with "main idea" questions, the teacher should: (Skill 10.4, Average Rigor)

A. Give out a strategy sheet on the main idea for children to place in their reader's notebooks.
B. Model responding to such a question as part of the guided reading.
C. Have children create "main idea questions" to go with their writings.
D. All of the above.

14. Making inferences from the text means that the reader: (Skill 10.4, Easy)

A. Is making informed judgments based on available evidence.
B. Is making a guess based on prior experiences.
C. Is making a guess based on what the reader would like to be true of the text.
D. All of the above.

15. Sometimes children can be asked to demonstrate their understanding of a text in a non-written format. This might include all of the following except: (Skill 10.4, Average Rigor)

A. A story map.
B. A Venn diagram.
C. Storyboarding a part of the story with dialogue bubbles.
D. Retelling or paraphrasing.

16. Which of the following is the least preferable strategy for teaching literature? (Skill 10.4, Rigorous)

A. Teacher-guided total class discussion
B. Small group discussion
C. Teacher lecture
D. Dramatization of literature selections

17. Which of the following is considered a study skill? (Skill 10.5, Average Rigor)

A. Using graphs, tables, and maps
B. Using a desk-top publishing program
C. Explaining important vocabulary words
D. Asking for clarification

18. A sixth-grade science teacher has given her class a paper to read on the relationship between food and weight gain. The writing contains signal words such as "because," "consequently," "this is how," and "due to." This paper has which text structure? (Skill 10.5, Rigorous)

A. cause & effect
B. compare & contrast
C. description
D. sequencing

19. Varying the complexity of a graphic organizer would be an example of differentiating: (Skill 11.1, Rigorous)

A. content/topic
B. environment
C. process
D. product

20. A student has written a paper with the following characteristics: written in first person; characters, setting, and plot; some dialogue; events organized in chronological sequence with some flashbacks. In what genre has the student written? (Skill 11.1, Rigorous)

A. expository writing
B. narrative writing
C. persuasive writing
D. technical writing

21. A technique used to allow students to present written ideas without interruption of the flow of thoughts is called: (Skill 11.1, Average Rigor)

A. brainstorming.
B. mapping.
C. listing.
D. Free writing.

22. Which of the following is not a technique of prewriting? (Skill 11.1, Easy)

A. Clustering
B. Listing
C. Brainstorming
D. Proofreading

23. If a student uses inappropriate language that includes slang and expletives, what is the best course of action to take in order to influence the student's formal communication skills? (Skill 11.2, Rigorous)

A. Ask the student to paraphrase the writing, that is, translate it into language appropriate for the school principal to read.
B. Refuse to read the student's papers until he conforms to a more literate style.
C. Ask the student to read his work aloud to the class for peer evaluation.
D. Rewrite the flagrant passages to show the student the right form of expression.

24. The practice of reading a piece of student writing to assess the overall impression of the product is: (Skill 11.2, Rigorous)

A. holistic evaluation.
B. portfolio assessment.
C. analytical evaluation.
D. using a performance system.

25. Of the following, which one is the Middle-School student most likely to be encountering for the first time? (Skill 11.4, Average Rigor)

A. Phonics.
B. Phonemics.
C. Textbook reading assignments.
D. Stories read by the teacher.

ANSWER KEY: INSTRUCTIONAL SUPPORT

1. c
2. a
3. c
4. b
5. c
6. b
7. b
8. d
9. c
10. c
11. c
12. d
13. d
14. a
15. d
16. c
17. a
18. a
19. c
20. b
21. d
22. d
23. a
24. a
25. c

RIGOR TABLE: INSTRUCTIONAL SUPPORT

Easy	Average Rigor	Rigorous
Question #s – 3, 4, 5, 14, 22	Question #s – 2, 6, 10, 11, 12, 13, 15, 17, 21, 25	Question #s – 1, 7, 8, 9, 16, 18, 19, 20, 23, 24

RATIONALES WITH SAMPLE QUESTIONS: **INSTRUCTIONAL SUPPORT**

1. The major difference between phonemic and phonological awareness is: (Skill 10.1, Rigorous)

A. One deals with a series of discrete sounds and sound spelling relationships.
B. One is involved with teaching and learning alliteration and rhymes.
C. Phonemic awareness is a specific type phonological awareness that deals with separate phonemes within a given word.
D. Phonological awareness is associated with printed words.

The answer is C. By definition, phonemic awareness falls under the phonological awareness umbrella. All of the other choices do not deal with the DIFFERENCE between the two types of awareness.

2. All of the following are true about phonological awareness EXCEPT: (Skill 10.1, Average Rigor)

A. It may involve print.
B. It is a prerequisite for spelling and phonics.
C. Activities can be done by the children with their eyes closed.
D. Starts before letter recognition is taught.

The answer is A. The key word here is EXCEPT which will be highlighted in upper case on the test as well. All of the options are correct aspects of phonological awareness except the first one, A, because phonological awareness DOES NOT involve print.

3. The best way for a primary grade teacher to model directionality and one to one word matching would be: (Skill 10.1, Easy)

A. Using a regular library or classroom text book.
B. Using her own person reading book.
C. Using a big book.
D. Using a book dummy.

The answer is C. Key word in this question is “best” and the answer is “C” because this type of a book is best for teaching and display.

4. To decode is to: (Skill 10.1, Easy)

A. Construct meaning.
B. Sound out a printed sequence of letters.
C. Use a special code to decipher a message.
D. None of the above.

The answer is B. Decoding is the process of sounding out the printed sequence of letters.

5. The word "bat" is a ___word for "batter-up": (Skill 10.1, Easy)

A. Suffix.
B. Prefix.
C. Root word.
D. Inflectional ending.

The answer is C. Root words are also known as base words and are the word without any additional affixes.

6. "Self correct" in reading means: (Skill 10.2, Average Rigor)

A. The teacher corrects on the record the errors the child makes.
B. The child goes back and corrects errors made in a running record.
C. The reading specialist teaches this to the child.
D. a and

The answer is B. This is a key principle of the running record and of keeping any reading record.

7. How could a KWL chart be used in instruction? (Skill 10.3, Rigorous)

A. To motivate students to do a research paper
B. To assess prior knowledge of the students
C. To assist in teaching skills
D. To put events in sequential order

The answer is B. To understand information, not simply repeat it, students must connect it to their previous understanding. Textbooks can't do that. Instead, teachers—the people who know students best—have to find out what they know and how to build on that knowledge. In science, having students make predictions before conducting experiments is an obvious way of finding out what they know, and having them compare their observations to those predictions helps connect new knowledge and old. In history, teachers can also ask students what they know about a topic before they begin studying it or ask them to make predictions about what they will learn. KWL charts, in which students discuss what they know, what they want to know, and (later) what they have learned, are one way to activate this prior knowledge.

8. Julia has been hired to work in a school that serves a local public housing project. She is working with kindergarten children and has been asked to focus on shared reading. She selects: (Skill 10.4, Rigorous)

A. Chapter books.
B. Riddle books.
C. Alphabet books.
D. Wordless picture books.

The answer is D. Given the fact this is a kindergarten in a public housing project, she will be most successful with wordless picture books, since there is no guarantee the children have had prior exposure to the other types of books listed. The answer "D" will allow them to construct a story from the pictures.

9. A teacher has taught his students several strategies to monitor their reading comprehension. These strategies include identifying where in the passage they are having difficulty, identifying what the difficulty is, and restating the difficult sentence or passage in their own words. These strategies are examples of: (Skill 10.4, Rigorous)

A. graphic and semantic organizers
B. metacognition
C. recognizing story structure
D. summarizing

The answer is C. Metacognition may be defined as "thinking about thinking." Good readers use metacognitive strategies to think about and have control over their reading. Before reading, they might clarify their purpose for reading and preview the text. During reading, they might monitor their understanding, adjusting their reading speed to fit the difficulty of the text and fixing any comprehension problems they have. After reading, they check their understanding of what they read.

10. Asking a child if what he or she has read makes sense to him or her, is prompting the child to use: (Skill 10.4, Average Rigor)

A. Phonics cues.
B. Syntactic cues.
C. Semantic cues.
D. Prior knowledge.

The answer is C. Semantic cues are the hints that students can discern from the reading to help them make sense of the text. In some cases, the message of the text depends on the other words around them, so students learn how to determine the meaning from context clues.

11. When you ask a child, if what he or she has just read "sounds right" to him or her, you are trying to get that child to use: (Skill 10.4, Average Rigor)

A. Phonics cues.
B. Syntactic cues.
C. Semantic cues.
D. Prior knowledge.

The answer is C. This is another one of those 'scripted" answers currently in use in reading. The answer has to be "B," syntactic clues.

12. As part of study about the agricultural products of their state, children have identified 22 different types of apples produced in the state. They can use a _______to compare and contrast these different types of apples: (Skill 10.4, Average Rigor)

A. Word web.
B. Semantic map.
C. Semantic features analysis grid.
D. All of the above.

The answer is D. The answer here is "D" and all of these graphic organizers would work with the apples.

13. To help children with "main idea" questions, the teacher should: (Skill 10.4, Average Rigor)

A. Give out a strategy sheet on the main idea for children to place in their reader's notebooks.
B. Model responding to such a question as part of the guided reading.
C. Have children create "main idea questions" to go with their writings.
D. All of the above.

The answer is D. This is one where all the options are right.

14. Making inferences from the text means that the reader: (Skill 10.4, Easy)

A. Is making informed judgments based on available evidence.
B. Is making a guess based on prior experiences.
C. Is making a guess based on what the reader would like to be true of the text.
D. All of the above.

The answer is A. This is a definition question that a literate test taker can answer based on the general definition of inferences.

15. Sometimes children can be asked to demonstrate their understanding of a text in a non-written format. This might include all of the following except: (Skill 10.4, Average Rigor)

A. A story map.
B. A Venn diagram.
C. Storyboarding a part of the story with dialogue bubbles.
D. Retelling or paraphrasing.

The answer is D. Retelling and paraphrasing can be in oral form whereas the other choices all involve writing or the use of pencil and paper. By asking students to retell a story, the teacher can determine the level of comprehension. Of course, this has to be modeled for the student, especially paraphrasing, so that the student relates the important facts or events and does not include any information that is not necessary.

16. Which of the following is the least preferable strategy for teaching literature? (Skill 10.4, Rigorous)

A. Teacher-guided total class discussion
B. Small group discussion
C. Teacher lecture
D. Dramatization of literature selections

The answer is C. In order to engage students' interest, it is necessary that they be involved whether through discussion or dramatization. A lecture is a much too passive technique to involve students of this age.

17. Which of the following is considered a study skill? (Skill 10.5, Average Rigor)

A. Using graphs, tables, and maps
B. Using a desk-top publishing program
C. Explaining important vocabulary words
D. Asking for clarification

The answer is A. In studying, it is certainly true that "a picture is worth a thousand words." Not only are these devices useful in making a point clear, they are excellent mnemonic devices for remembering facts.

18. A sixth-grade science teacher has given her class a paper to read on the relationship between food and weight gain. The writing contains signal words such as "because," "consequently," "this is how," and "due to." This paper has which text structure? (Skill 10.5, Rigorous)

A. cause & effect
B. compare & contrast
C. description
D. sequencing

The answer is A. Cause and effect is the relationship between two things when one thing makes something else happen. Writers use this text structure to show order, inform, speculate, and change behavior. This text structure uses the process of identifying potential causes of a problem or issue in an orderly way. It is often used to teach social studies and science concepts. It is characterized by signal words such as because, so, so that, if... then, consequently, thus, since, for, for this reason, as a result of, therefore, due to, this is how, nevertheless, and accordingly.

19. Varying the complexity of a graphic organizer would be an example of differentiating: (Skill 11.1, Rigorous)

A. content/topic
B. environment
C. process
D. product

The answer is C. Differentiating the processes means varying learning activities or strategies to provide appropriate methods for students to explore the concepts. It is important to give students alternative paths to manipulate the ideas embedded within the concept. For example, students may use graphic organizers, maps, diagrams, or charts to display their comprehension of concepts covered. Varying the complexity of the graphic organizer can very effectively facilitate differing levels of cognitive processing for students of differing ability.

20. A student has written a paper with the following characteristics: written in first person; characters, setting, and plot; some dialogue; events organized in chronological sequence with some flashbacks. In what genre has the student written? (Skill 11.1, Rigorous)

A. expository writing
B. narrative writing
C. persuasive writing
D. technical writing

The answer is B. These are all characteristics of narrative writing. Expository writing is intended to give information such as an explanation or directions, and the information is logically organized. Persuasive writing gives an opinion in an attempt to convince the reader that this point of view is valid or tries to persuade the reader to take a specific action. The goal of technical writing is to clearly communicate a select piece of information to a targeted reader or group of readers for a particular purpose in such a way that the subject can readily be understood. It is persuasive writing that anticipates a response from the reader.

21. A technique used to allow students to present written ideas without interruption of the flow of thoughts is called: (Skill 11.1, Average Rigor)

A. brainstorming.
B. mapping.
C. listing.
D. Free writing.

The answer is D. Free writing fourteen or fifteen minutes allows the student to write out his/her thoughts about a subject. This technique allows the student to develop ideas s/he is conscious of, but it also helps him/her develop ideas that belong to the subconscious. It is important to let the flow of ideas run through the hand. If the student gets stuck, s/he can write the last sentence over again until inspiration comes back.

22. Which of the following is not a technique of prewriting? (Skill 11.1, Easy)

A. Clustering
B. Listing
C. Brainstorming
D. Proofreading

The answer is D. Proofreading should be reserved for the final draft.

23. If a student uses inappropriate language that includes slang and expletives, what is the best course of action to take in order to influence the student's formal communication skills? (Skill 11.2, Rigorous)

A. Ask the student to paraphrase the writing, that is, translate it into language appropriate for the school principal to read.
B. Refuse to read the student's papers until he conforms to a more literate style.
C. Ask the student to read his work aloud to the class for peer evaluation.
D. Rewrite the flagrant passages to show the student the right form of expression.

The answer is A. Asking the student to write for a specific audience will help him become more involved in his writing. If he continues writing to the same audience—the teacher—he will continue seeing writing as just another assignment and he will not apply grammar, vocabulary, and syntax the way they should be. By paraphrasing his own writing, the student will learn to write for a different public.

24. The practice of reading a piece of student writing to assess the overall impression of the product is: (Skill 11.2, Rigorous)

A. holistic evaluation.
B. portfolio assessment.
C. analytical evaluation.
D. using a performance system.

The answer is A. Holistic Scoring assesses a piece of writing as a whole. Usually a paper is read quickly through once to get a general impression. The writing is graded according to the impression of the whole work rather than the sum of its parts. Often holistic scoring uses a rubric that establishes the overall criteria for a certain score to evaluate each paper.

25. Of the following, which one is the Middle-School student most likely to be encountering for the first time? (Skill 11.4, Average Rigor)

A. Phonics.
B. Phonemics.
C. Textbook reading assignments.
D. Stories read by the teacher.

The answer is C. For the first time, the student will be expected to read textbook assignments and come to class prepared to discuss the content.

XAMonline, INC. 21 Orient Ave. Melrose, MA 02176

Toll Free number 800-509-4128

TO ORDER Fax 781-662-9268 OR www.XAMonline.com

GEORGIA ASSESSMENTS FOR THE CERTIFICATION OF EDUCATORS -GACE - 2008

P0# Store/School:

Address 1:

Address 2 (Ship to other):

City, State Zip

Credit card number______-_______-________-_______ expiration_______

EMAIL ______________________________

PHONE **FAX**

13# ISBN 2007	TITLE	Qty	Retail	Total
978-1-58197-257-3	Basic Skills 200, 201, 202			
978-1-58197-528-4	Biology 026, 027			
978-1-58197-584-0	Science 024, 025			
978-1-58197-341-9	English 020, 021			
978-1-58197-569-7	Physics 030, 031			
978-1-58197-531-4	Art Education Sample Test 109, 110			
978-1-58197-545-1	History 034, 035			
978-1-58197-527-7	Health and Physical Education 115, 116			
978-1-58197-540-6	Chemistry 028, 029			
978-1-58197-534-5	Reading 117, 118			
978-1-58197-547-5	Media Specialist 101, 102			
978-1-58197-535-2	Middle Grades Reading 012			
978-1-58197-591-8	Middle Grades Science 014			
978-1-58197-345-7	Middle Grades Mathematics 013			
978-1-58197-686-1	Middle Grades Social Science 015			
978-158-197-598-7	Middle Grades Language Arts 011			
978-1-58197-346-4	Mathematics 022, 023			
978-1-58197-549-9	Political Science 032, 033			
978-1-58197-588-8	Paraprofessional Assessment 177			
978-1-58197-589-5	Professional Pedagogy Assessment 171, 172			
978-1-58197-259-7	Early Childhood Education 001, 002			
978-1-58197-587-1	School Counseling 103, 104			
978-1-58197-541-3	Spanish 141, 142			
978-1-58197-610-6	Special Education General Curriculum 081, 082			
978-1-58197-530-7	French Sample Test 143, 144			
			SUBTOTAL	
FOR PRODUCT PRICES GO TO WWW.XAMONLINE.COM			**Ship**	$8.25
			TOTAL	

CPSIA information can be obtained
at www.ICGtesting.com
Printed in the USA
LVHW060151270323
742678LV00012B/386